Merry Christmas
Mommie —
With all my love
1998
Daddy

QUICK FROM SCRATCH

Fish & Shellfish

Orange Roughy on Rice with Thai-Spiced Coconut Sauce, page 165

QUICK FROM SCRATCH
Fish & Shellfish

American Express Publishing Corporation
New York

Editor in Chief: Judith Hill
Associate Editor: Susan Lantzius
Assistant Editor: Laura Byrne Russell
Managing Editor: Terri Mauro
Copy Editor: Barbara A. Mateer
Wine Editor: Richard Marmet
Art Director: Nina Scerbo
Editorial Assistant: Evette Manners
Photographer: Melanie Acevedo
Food Stylist: Rori Spinelli
Prop Stylist: Robyn Glaser
Production Manager: Yvette Williams-Braxton

Vice President, Books and Information Services: John Stoops
Marketing Director: David Geller
Marketing/Promotion Manager: Roni Stein
Operations Manager: Doreen Camardi
Business Manager: Joanne Ragazzo

Recipes Pictured on Cover: (Front) Salmon with Red-Wine Sauce, page 51
(Back) Grilled Shrimp with Couscous Salad, page 177;
Inset top: Orange and Fennel Roasted Cod, page 43;
Inset bottom: Crab Cakes with Horseradish Cream, page 111
Page 6: *Kitchen photo:* Bill Bettencourt; *Portraits:* Christopher Dinerman

Pages 23, 97, 101, 117, and 171: Recipes contributed by Andrew Rosenkranz

AMERICAN EXPRESS PUBLISHING CORPORATION
©1997 American Express Publishing Corporation

LIBRARY OF CONGRESS CATALOGING-IN-PUBLICATION DATA
Quick from scratch. Fish & Shellfish.
p.   cm.
Includes bibliographical references and index.
ISBN 0-916103-38-2
1. Cookery (Fish) 2. Cookery (Shellfish)   I. Food & wine (New York, N.Y.)
TX747.Q57   1997
641.6'92—dc21   97-15944
                                                                CIP

Published by American Express Publishing Corporation
1120 Avenue of the Americas, New York, New York 10036

Manufactured in the United States of America

CONTENTS

RECIPES PICTURED ABOVE: *(left to right)* pages 73, 161, 105

Working on shellfish recipes at FOOD & WINE Books

Susan Lantzius trained at La Varenne École de Cuisine in Paris, worked as a chef in Portugal for a year, and then headed to New York City. There she made her mark first as head decorator at the well-known Sant Ambroeus pastry shop and next as a pastry chef, working at such top restaurants as San Domenico and Maxim's. In 1993, she turned her talents to recipe development and editorial work for FOOD & WINE Books.

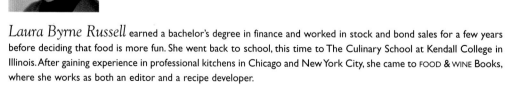

Judith Hill is the editor in chief of FOOD & WINE Books, a division of American Express Publishing. Previously she was editor in chief of COOK'S Magazine, director of publications for La Varenne École de Cuisine in Paris, from which she earned a Grand Diplôme, and an English instructor for the University of Maryland International Division in Germany. Her book credits include editing cookbooks for Fredy Girardet, Jane Grigson, Michel Guérard, and Anne Willan.

Laura Byrne Russell earned a bachelor's degree in finance and worked in stock and bond sales for a few years before deciding that food is more fun. She went back to school, this time to The Culinary School at Kendall College in Illinois. After gaining experience in professional kitchens in Chicago and New York City, she came to FOOD & WINE Books, where she works as both an editor and a recipe developer.

INTRODUCTION

You, our readers who have enjoyed other books in this series, have told us that you want this particular volume—that you'd like to serve fish but don't quite feel comfortable with it as an ingredient and need some good ideas for cooking it. Your requests launched us (Susan Lantzius, Laura Russell, and I), and we have had more fun writing this book than any other that FOOD & WINE Books has published so far. We often felt as though we were playing rather than working. For one thing, fish is almost never cooked more than a few minutes, and so coming up with ideas for quick dishes wasn't hard.

Because so many different combinations of texture and flavor exist among fish and because each variety can be prepared so many different ways, we didn't feel as though we were eating the same thing day after day. In fact, our tasting sessions were a treat. During the months that we worked perfecting our ideas into recipes, often sampling dishes in various stages of development eight or ten times a day, none of the three of us tired of fish. I was stunned to find myself ordering fish even when I went out to a restaurant.

Another thing that made working on this book so easy is that fish, despite their diversity, are amazingly interchangeable. On page 10, we include a chart that details fish to substitute for the ones we specify in the recipes. The fish suggested as replacements have characteristics that are similar to those of the original choices—juicy or dry, oily or lean, flaky or dense, strong or mild. However, you can often substitute a fish with an entirely *different* identity. The **Crab Cakes with Horseradish Cream** (page 111) are delectable made with the sweet shellfish, but exactly the same recipe is wonderful, though quite different, made with mild, flaky cod. We used a firm, gelatinous, mild, and lean fish in **Pan-Roasted Monkfish with Mushrooms and Scallions** (page 47), and then discovered that full-flavored salmon, with its entirely different texture and oil content, is delicious made in just the same way. We've noted such unexpected, out-of-the-family replacements throughout the book. No matter where you live, whatever your regional fish, you should be able to use all the recipes here.

Quick-cooking, varied, versatile fish—here's your book on the subject, as requested. We hope you enjoy using it as much as we did making it.

Judith Hill
Editor in Chief
FOOD & WINE Books

Before You Begin

You'll find test-kitchen tips and ideas for ingredient substitutions presented with the individual recipes throughout the book. In this opening section, we've gathered information and tips that apply to all, or at least a substantial number, of the recipes. These are the facts and opinions that we'd like you to know before you use the recipes and to keep in mind while you use them. We hope you'll read these pages prior to cooking from the book for the first time—and have kept the section short so that you can do so with ease. The culinary information here will help make your cooking quicker, simpler, and even tastier.

RECIPES PICTURED OPPOSITE: (top) pages 71, 141, 55; (center) pages 109, 25, 91; (bottom) pages 67, 175, 53.

Fish Substitutions

If the fish called for in one of our recipes is out of season or unavailable in your area, you can certainly substitute another one. First, look for the fish the recipe specifies in column three below. You'll find a fish of similar texture and flavor by either choosing another one in the same grouping in column three or selecting one of the substitutions in column four. Every fish has its own unique characteristics, so the dish will be slightly different—but no less delicious. Use this chart as a guide, not a rule book. In many cases, you can even substitute a fish with completely different qualities, as we've noted in the individual recipes.

TEXTURE	FLAVOR	FOR ANY OF THESE	SUBSTITUTE ANY OF THESE
Relatively soft	mild	sole, such as gray or lemon, and other flounder trout	croaker drum fluke freshwater bass hake lake perch sand dab walleye whiting
Relatively soft	full	bluefish mackerel shad	kingfish porgy
Relatively soft	full	sardines	other small, whole fish, such as anchovies and smelts
Medium firm	mild	**Large flake** cod/scrod halibut orange roughy	blackfish Chilean sea bass haddock pollack turbot

Texture	Flavor	Fish	See individual recipes
Medium flake		grouper, red snapper, sea bass, skate, tilapia	black cod/sablefish, black sea bass, John Dory, ocean perch, pike, pompano, rockfish, striped bass, tilefish, wolffish
Medium firm to firm	mild	catfish	see individual recipes
Medium firm	full	salmon	char
Firm	mild	mahimahi, shark, swordfish	marlin, sturgeon
Firm	mild	monkfish	see individual recipes
Firm	full	tuna	mahimahi, marlin, shark, sturgeon, swordfish

ESSENTIAL INGREDIENT INFORMATION

Broth, Chicken
We tested the recipes in this book with canned low-sodium chicken broth. You can almost always substitute regular for low-sodium broth; just cut back on the salt in the recipe. And if you keep home-made stock in your freezer, by all means feel free to use it. We aren't suggesting that it won't work as well, only that we know the dishes taste delicious even when made with canned broth.

Butter
Our recipes don't specify whether to use salted or unsalted butter. We generally use unsalted, but in these savory dishes, it really won't make a big difference which type you use.

Clam Juice, Bottled
Often a fine substitute for fish stock, bottled clam juice is simply the natural liquor from shucked clams. As with other store-bought broths, clam juice can be quite salty. Therefore, we often dilute it with water or another liquid.

Coconut Milk
Coconut milk is the traditional liquid used in many Thai and Indian curries. Make sure you buy *unsweetened* canned coconut milk, not cream of coconut, which is used primarily for piña coladas. Heavy cream can be substituted in many recipes.

Garlic
The size of garlic cloves varies tremendously. When we call for one minced or chopped clove, we expect you to get about three-quarters of a teaspoon.

Ginger, Fresh
Fresh ginger, or ginger root, is a knobby, tan-skinned rhizome found in the produce section of your supermarket. You need to peel its thin skin before using; this is most easily accomplished by scraping it with a spoon. After peeling, the ginger is ready to be grated, sliced, or chopped.

Mustard
When we call for mustard, we mean Dijon or grainy. We never, ever mean yellow ballpark mustard.

Oil

Cooking oil in these recipes refers to readily available, reasonably priced nut, seed, or vegetable oil with a high smoking point, such as peanut, sunflower, canola, safflower, or corn oil. These can be heated to about 400° before they begin to smoke, break down, and develop an unpleasant flavor.

Parsley

Many of our recipes call for chopped fresh parsley. The flat-leaf variety has a stronger flavor than the curly, and we use it most of the time, but unless the type is specified, you can use either.

Pepper

■ There's nothing like fresh-ground pepper. If you've been using preground, buy a pepper mill, fill it, and give it a grind. You'll never look back.

■ To measure your just-ground pepper more easily, become familiar with your own mill; each produces a different amount per turn. You'll probably find that ten to fifteen grinds produces one-quarter teaspoon of pepper, and then you can count on that forever after.

Tomatoes, Canned

In some recipes, we call for "crushed tomatoes in thick puree." Depending on the brand, this mix of crushed tomatoes and tomato puree may be labeled crushed tomatoes with puree, with added puree, in tomato puree, thick style, or in thick puree. You can use any of these.

Wine, Dry White

Leftover wine is ideal for cooking. It seems a shame to open a fresh bottle for just a few spoonfuls. Another solution is to keep dry vermouth on hand. You can use whatever quantity is needed; the rest will keep indefinitely.

Zest

Citrus zest—the colored part of the peel, without any of the white pith—adds tremendous flavor to many a dish. Remove the zest from the fruit using either a grater or a zester. A zester is a small, inexpensive, and extremely handy tool. It has little holes that remove just the zest in fine ribbons. A zester is quick, easy to clean, and never scrapes your knuckles.

Faster, Better, Easier
Test-Kitchen Tips

Choosing for Freshness

Fresh fish gleams; it should fairly call out to you to take it home. In the shop, it should be resting on a cooling bed of crushed ice, and the smell should be sweet, clean, and, for sea fish, briny—never fishy. To make sure you bring home the highest quality fish, look for:

Whole Fish
- shiny skin
- firm, springy flesh
- bright red gills
- convex rather than sunken eyes

Steaks and Fillets
- moist skin
- consistent color and texture with no signs of browning or gaping
- a plump rather than dehydrated look

Storing Raw Fish

Fish is best when cooked on the day you buy it. If, however, you want to keep it for a day or two, rinse the fish, dry it with paper towels, and wrap it in plastic. Then, ideally, put the fish in a colander set over a shallow pan, and cover the fish with crushed ice. It will stay cold enough to slow its decline, and the pan will collect the water as the ice melts. Or, keep the fish in the coldest part of the refrigerator. It's a good idea to rinse the fish and dry it again after a day.

Freezing Fish

Although impeccably fresh fish is always the tastiest, well-wrapped steaks and fillets can be frozen for at least three months (for oil-rich fish) and as long as six months (for lean fish). Among shellfish, only shrimp, squid, and crawfish can be frozen successfully; six months is the limit for these, too. The best way to defrost frozen fish is in the refrigerator, but if you're pressed for time, putting the still-wrapped package in a bowl of cold water will do the trick.

Good Skin

Crisp, **panfried** skin has great appeal. Many fish, such as trout, salmon, and red snapper, have skin that's good to eat, so you'll want to be sure the fish are scaled. **Braising and poaching**, however, make the skin flabby and unappetizing; you'll probably prefer to ignore it when it's been cooked by a moist-heat method.

Scaling Fish

If you purchase fish steaks, fillets, or a whole, cleaned fish, chances are the scales have been removed. If they haven't been, simply hold the fish under cold running water while scraping the scales off with the back (dull side) of a knife.

Quick, Flavorful Shrimp Stock

When clam juice or chicken broth are called for in shrimp recipes, you can make a flavorful stock from the shells to use instead. Buy unpeeled shrimp, shell them, and then put the shells in a medium saucepan with enough water to cover. Bring the mixture just to a boil, reduce the heat and let simmer for about ten minutes. Strain before using.

Cook until Golden Brown

To ensure browning when using a dry-heat method, such as grilling, roasting, or sautéing, be sure to:

- dry the fish thoroughly with paper towels
- get the pan, oven, or grill really hot before adding the fish
- for sautéing and frying, use an oil that can take the heat, such as corn, peanut, or safflower, rather than olive

Grilling

To grill fish and shellfish to perfection without it sticking or falling through the grate:

- start with a clean grill
- lightly oil firm fish fillets and steaks and turn them only once during grilling
- invest in a grill topper (sheet of perforated metal) for delicate fillets and whole fish
- use a grill topper or skewers for shrimp and scallops

Adjusting Cooking Times

In each recipe, we've given cooking times for fish fillets and steaks of a specific thickness. If your fish is thicker or thinner, add or subtract a few minutes from the cooking time.

Testing Fish for Doneness

For optimum flavor and moistness, cook most fish just until cooked through. Avoid overcooking; even a minute of extra time can result in dry fish. To test for doneness, make a small cut in the thickest part of the flesh with the tip of a paring knife; the flesh should be opaque. That is, unless you're cooking salmon and tuna. Salmon is juiciest when the flesh is almost cooked through but still translucent in the very center. We think tuna is most delicious cooked to medium rare, when the flesh is opaque around the edge but most of the meat is still red and translucent.

Soups
&
Stews

Minestrone with Sole

Thick and chunky with vegetables and pieces of sole, this pesto-flavored soup is hearty enough to make a meal. Serve it hot to take the chill off a winter night, or at room temperature for a cool summertime supper.

WINE RECOMMENDATION

A light Italian white wine will be delightful with the vegetables and pesto. Look for the most recent vintage of a pinot grigio from the northern Alto Adige region.

SERVES 4

- 1 tablespoon butter
- 3 tablespoons olive oil
- 1 onion, chopped
- 2 cloves garlic, minced
- 2 carrots, cut into ¼-inch dice
- 2 ribs celery, cut into ¼-inch dice
- ¾ pound boiling potatoes (about 2), peeled and cut into ¼-inch dice
- 1 zucchini, cut into ¼-inch dice
- ¼ head cabbage (about ¾ pound), shredded
- 3¾ cups canned low-sodium chicken broth or homemade stock
- 1½ cups drained and rinsed canned pinto beans (one 15-ounce can)
- 1 tablespoon tomato paste
- 1½ teaspoons salt
- 1½ pounds sole fillets, cut into 1-inch pieces
- 2 tablespoons pesto, store-bought or homemade
- ¼ teaspoon fresh-ground black pepper

1. In a large pot, melt the butter with the oil over moderate heat. Add the onion and cook, stirring occasionally, until golden, about 5 minutes. Add the garlic, carrots, celery, and potatoes and cook, stirring occasionally, for 5 minutes. Add the zucchini and cabbage and cook, stirring occasionally, for 5 minutes longer.

2. Add the broth, beans, tomato paste, and salt and bring to a simmer. Simmer, partially covered, until the vegetables are tender, about 18 minutes. Add the sole, pesto, and pepper and bring back to a simmer. Cook, uncovered, until the fish is just done, about 1 to 2 minutes more. To serve, ladle into bowls and pass more pesto if you like.

Fish Alternatives

You can use any other member of the flounder family, such as sand dab or fluke, in place of the sole. Or try a firmer, white fish, such as cod, halibut, or monkfish. For these thicker fish, add another minute to the cooking time.

THAI HOT-AND-SOUR FISH SOUP

In our hot-and-sour soup, lemon and lime zest, lime juice, and fresh ginger replace the traditional lemongrass, kaffir lime leaves, and galangal, which can be difficult to find. To change the heat level, adjust the number of jalapeños up or down to your taste.

WINE RECOMMENDATION
The strong flavors here suggest a light white without too much taste of its own. A pinot grigio from Italy will do fine—unless you increase the heat with more jalapeños. Then serve a cold beer.

SERVES 4

1½ tablespoons cooking oil

3 shallots, cut into thin slices

1 tablespoon chopped fresh ginger

5 jalapeño peppers, seeds and ribs removed, peppers cut into thin slices

1 quart canned low-sodium chicken broth or homemade stock

2 cups water

Grated zest of 2 lemons

Grated zest of 3 limes

½ pound mushrooms, quartered

5 tablespoons lime juice (from about 3 limes)

¼ cup Asian fish sauce (nam pla or nuoc mam)*

2 pounds swordfish steaks, skinned, cut into approximately 2-by-1-inch pieces

2 tomatoes, cut into large dice (optional)

⅓ cup cilantro leaves (optional)

*Available at Asian markets and many supermarkets

1. In a large pot, heat the oil over moderately low heat. Add the shallots, ginger, and jalapeños; cook, stirring occasionally, for 3 minutes. Add the broth and water; bring to a boil. Reduce the heat and simmer for 5 minutes. Stir in the zests and mushrooms; simmer 5 minutes longer.

2. Add the lime juice, fish sauce, and swordfish to the soup. Cook until the fish is just done, about 2 minutes. Serve sprinkled with the tomatoes and cilantro, if using.

FISH ALTERNATIVES

Thai Hot-and-Sour Soup is often made with shrimp. Or, use any moderately firm, skinless steaks or fillets, such as catfish, black sea bass, or pompano, in place of the swordfish.

ASIAN FISH SAUCE

Fish sauce is used as a condiment, much like soy sauce. Either the Thai version (nam pla) or the Vietnamese (nuoc mam) will add great depth of flavor to quick dishes.

CORN-AND-COD CHOWDER

With its all-American ingredients, this New England-style chowder is a comfort-food classic. The soup needs only bread, or traditional oyster crackers, as an accompaniment.

WINE RECOMMENDATION
A rich chardonnay from California will pair nicely with the creaminess of the chowder. Try to find one that hasn't been aged in oak.

SERVES 4

- ¼ pound sliced bacon
- 1 tablespoon butter
- 2 onions, chopped
- 2 cups water
- 1 cup bottled clam juice
- ¾ pound boiling potatoes (about 2), peeled and cut into ¾-inch chunks
- 1 rib celery, chopped
- ¼ teaspoon dried red-pepper flakes
- 1¼ teaspoons salt
- 2 cups fresh (cut from about 3 ears) or frozen corn kernels
- 1 cup milk
- 1 cup heavy cream
- 1½ pounds cod fillets, cut into 1½-inch chunks
- ¼ teaspoon fresh-ground black pepper

1. In a large pot, cook the bacon until crisp. Drain the bacon on paper towels and crumble when cooled.

2. Add the butter and onions to the pot. Cook over moderately low heat, stirring occasionally, until the onions are translucent, about 5 minutes.

3. Add the water, clam juice, potatoes, celery, red-pepper flakes, and salt and bring to a boil. Reduce the heat and simmer until the potatoes are tender, about 20 minutes.

4. Return the bacon to the pot. Add the corn, milk, and cream and simmer for 10 minutes. Stir in the cod and pepper. Bring back to a simmer and cook until just done, about 3 minutes longer.

FISH ALTERNATIVES

Use a relatively firm, mild fish that won't disintegrate in the soup, such as pollack, orange roughy, or ocean perch.

CURRIED CARROT AND MUSSEL SOUP

Two shortcuts are at work here to make a simple, yet satisfying bowl of soup. To add body without adding loads of time for the soup to cook down, simply puree half of it and stir this back into the pot. And to give the soup extra flavor without extra effort, steam the mussels in white wine and use the liquid as a simple seafood stock.

WINE RECOMMENDATION
The perfect choice with curry spices is a refreshing acidic white wine. Try a bottle of the classic shellfish wine, Muscadet de Sèvre-et-Maine from the Loire Valley in France.

SERVES 4

- 4 tablespoons butter
- 2 onions, cut into thin slices
- 1¼ pounds carrots, cut into ¼-inch slices
- 1 tablespoon curry powder
- 1 quart canned low-sodium chicken broth or homemade stock
- 2 cups water
- 6 pounds small mussels, scrubbed and debearded
- 1 cup dry white wine
- 1¼ teaspoons salt

1. In a large pot, melt the butter over moderately low heat. Add the onions and carrots; cook, stirring occasionally, until the onions are translucent, about 5 minutes. Add the curry powder and cook, stirring, for 1 minute. Add the broth and water. Bring to a boil. Reduce the heat; simmer until the carrots are tender, about 10 minutes.

2. Discard any mussels that are broken or do not clamp shut when tapped. Put the wine and the mussels in a large stainless-steel pot. Cover and bring to a boil. Cook, shaking the pot occasionally, just until the mussels open, about 3 minutes. Remove the open mussels. Continue to boil, uncovering the pot as necessary to remove the mussels as soon as their shells open. Discard any that do not open. When the mussels are cool enough to handle, remove all but twelve of them from their shells, holding them over the pot to catch all the juices.

3. Puree half of the carrot mixture in a blender or food processor. Return the puree to the soup pot and stir in the salt. Carefully pour the mussel-cooking liquid into the soup, leaving any grit in the bottom of the pot. Add the shelled mussels to the soup and cook over low heat just until warmed through, about 1 minute. Serve the soup topped with the reserved mussels in their shells.

Tunisian Fish-and-Vegetable Stew

Carrots, turnip, zucchini, potatoes, and cod simmer in a spicy tomato broth redolent of garlic and cumin. The spiciness here comes from red-pepper flakes, but feel free to use the fiery Tunisian hot sauce *harissa* if you can get hold of some. Serve the fragrant stew with steamed couscous, which will absorb the generous quantity of broth.

WINE RECOMMENDATION

Serve a cold glass of rosé with this Mediterranean-inspired dish. Try Côtes de Provence or Bandol, both from France, or one of the new drier rosés from California.

SERVES 4

- 2 tablespoons cooking oil
- 1 onion, chopped
- 4 cloves garlic, cut into thin slices
- 3 tablespoons tomato paste
- 1½ teaspoons cumin
- ¼ teaspoon dried red-pepper flakes
- ½ teaspoon fresh-ground black pepper
- 1 teaspoon salt
- 1 quart canned low-sodium chicken broth or homemade stock
- ¾ pound boiling potatoes (about 2), peeled and cut into 1-inch pieces
- 3 carrots, cut into 1-inch pieces
- 1 turnip, peeled and cut into 1-inch pieces
- 2 zucchini, cut into 1-inch pieces
- 1½ pounds cod fillets, cut into 1½-inch chunks
- 3 tablespoons chopped fresh parsley

1. In a large pot, heat the oil over moderately low heat. Add the onion and garlic and cook, stirring occasionally, until the onion is translucent, about 5 minutes. Stir in the tomato paste, cumin, red-pepper flakes, black pepper, and ½ teaspoon of the salt. Cook, stirring, for 2 minutes.

2. Add the broth and bring to a simmer. Add the potatoes and carrots and simmer for 10 minutes. Stir in the turnip, zucchini, and the remaining ½ teaspoon salt. Simmer for 10 minutes longer. Add the cod, bring back to a simmer, and cook until just done, about 3 minutes. Serve the stew topped with the parsley.

Fish Alternatives

Any relatively firm, white-fleshed fish will work well. Try rockfish, grouper, or for a special treat, halibut. Be sure to remove the skin before adding the fish to the pot.

CREOLE CATFISH STEW

Chock-full of lima beans, corn, and chunks of catfish, this Creole-seasoned stew is a Southern delight. The heat level is moderate, but you can increase the spiciness by adding more Tabasco sauce or a bit of cayenne pepper.

WINE RECOMMENDATION
A light white wine, such as a pinot gris from Oregon or a seyval blanc from the eastern United States, will provide a refreshing counterpoint to the full flavor of the stew.

SERVES 4

2   tablespoons cooking oil

1   onion, chopped

2   ribs celery, cut into ½-inch slices

1   green bell pepper, cut into ½-inch strips

1   teaspoon dried thyme

½   teaspoon dried oregano

½   teaspoon dry mustard

½   teaspoon Tabasco sauce

½   teaspoon fresh-ground black pepper

1   teaspoon salt

½   cup dry white wine

1¾ cups canned crushed tomatoes in thick puree

3   cups canned low-sodium chicken broth or homemade stock

2   cups frozen baby lima beans (one 10-ounce package)

2   cups fresh (cut from about 3 ears) or frozen corn kernels

2   pounds catfish fillets, cut into 1½-inch pieces

2   tablespoons chopped fresh parsley

1. In a large pot, heat the oil over moderate heat. Add the onion, celery, and bell pepper and cook, stirring occasionally, until the onion is translucent, about 5 minutes. Stir in the thyme, oregano, mustard, Tabasco sauce, pepper, and ½ teaspoon of the salt. Add the wine and cook until almost evaporated, about 4 minutes.

2. Add the tomatoes and broth to the pot and bring to a boil. Reduce the heat and simmer, partially covered, for 10 minutes. Add the lima beans and simmer for 3 minutes. Stir in the corn and simmer 4 minutes more. Add the catfish and the remaining ½ teaspoon salt, bring back to a simmer, and cook until just done, about 2 minutes. Serve topped with the parsley.

FISH ALTERNATIVES

Catfish has a firm texture all its own, but you can easily substitute moderately firm, white-fleshed fillets such as rockfish, grouper, pollack, and striped bass.

GOAN CURRIED-FISH STEW

From Goa, a tropical area on the southern coast of India where coco palms are plentiful and fresh seafood abundant, comes this fish stew flavored with hot peppers, lemon juice, and coconut milk. Goans use a local flatfish called *pomfret*, similar to our sole, and serve the stew with plenty of rice. If you've never tried Goan cuisine, this is the place to start. The stew is delectable.

WINE RECOMMENDATION

The spiciness and creaminess of this stew will be best accompanied by either beer or a bottle of acidic white wine with enough flavor to stand up to the coconut milk and heat. Try a Vouvray or other wine made from chenin blanc from the Loire Valley in France.

SERVES 4

2 pounds sole fillets, cut into 1-inch pieces

¼ cup lemon juice (from about 1 lemon)

1¼ teaspoons salt

2 cloves garlic, smashed

4 teaspoons chopped fresh ginger

1 cup canned unsweetened coconut milk

1 tablespoon ground coriander

1 teaspoon ground cumin

1 teaspoon brown sugar

½ teaspoon fresh-ground black pepper

¼ teaspoon turmeric

⅛ teaspoon cayenne

3 tablespoons cooking oil

1 onion, chopped

1 tomato, chopped

4 jalapeño peppers, seeds and ribs removed, minced

¾ cup water

1. In a glass or stainless-steel container, combine the sole, lemon juice, and ½ teaspoon of the salt. Let marinate at least 10 minutes.

2. In a blender, puree the garlic and ginger with the coconut milk, coriander, cumin, brown sugar, black pepper, turmeric, and cayenne.

3. In a large saucepan, heat the oil over moderate heat. Add the onion; cook, stirring occasionally, until golden, about 5 minutes. Add the tomato and cook, stirring occasionally, until soft, about 5 minutes. Add the coconut mixture, the jalapeños, the water, and the remaining ¾ teaspoon salt and bring slowly almost to a simmer, stirring frequently.

4. Add the fish and 1 tablespoon of the marinade. Bring to a simmer and continue simmering until the fish is just done, 1 to 2 minutes.

COD-AND-CLAM AVGOLEMONO STEW

A lemony sauce coats rice, clams, and cod in this delicious version of a traditional Greek favorite. If the rice soaks up all of the sauce, add a little more chicken stock.

The aggressive, grassy flavor and sprightly acidity found in most sauvignon blancs will work well with the assertive dill here. A Sancerre or other sauvignon-blanc-based wine from elsewhere in France's Loire Valley is a good choice.

SERVES 4

3 cups canned low-sodium chicken broth or homemade stock, more if needed

1 onion, chopped

2 carrots, cut into 1/4-inch dice

1 1/2 teaspoons dried dill

1/3 cup rice

16 littleneck clams, scrubbed

1/2 cup water

1 1/2 pounds cod fillets, cut into 1-inch pieces

1 cup frozen petite peas

2 teaspoons salt

1/4 teaspoon fresh-ground black pepper

3 large eggs

3 tablespoons lemon juice

1. In a large saucepan, combine the broth, onion, carrots, and dill. Bring to a boil and cook, partially covered, over moderately low heat for 5 minutes. Stir in the rice and continue cooking, partially covered, until the rice is just done, about 15 minutes.

2. Discard any clams that are broken or do not clamp shut when tapped. Put the clams and water into a medium saucepan. Cover and bring to a boil over high heat. Cook, shaking the pot occasionally, just until the clams open, about 3 minutes. Remove the open clams and continue to cook, uncovering the saucepan as necessary to remove the clams as soon as their shells open. Discard any that do not open.

3. Carefully pour the clam-cooking liquid into the rice mixture, leaving any grit in the bottom of the saucepan. Add the fish, peas, salt, and pepper; bring to a simmer. If necessary, add more of the chicken broth to just cover the fish. Simmer, uncovered, until the fish is just done, about 2 minutes.

4. In a medium stainless-steel bowl, whisk together the eggs and lemon juice until frothy. Pour most of the hot liquid from the fish stew in a thin stream into the egg mixture, whisking. Pour the egg mixture back into the saucepan, stirring gently so as not to break up the fish. Gently stir in the clams in their shells.

CATAPLANA STEW WITH SAUSAGE AND CLAMS

Portuguese *cataplana* is a long-simmered pork stew to which clams are added. For our quick take on the dish, we've replaced the usual pork shoulder with sausage.

WINE RECOMMENDATION

Try this rustic Portuguese-style stew with that most basic and refreshing of Portuguese white wines, a vinho verde. Look for the youngest bottle you can find.

SERVES 4

1	tablespoon olive oil
1½	pounds mild Italian sausage
1	onion, chopped
2	cloves garlic, minced
1	teaspoon paprika
2	tablespoons tomato paste
½	cup bottled clam juice
½	cup dry white wine
2	bay leaves
	Pinch dried red-pepper flakes
16	littleneck clams, scrubbed
3	tablespoons chopped flat-leaf parsley
	Salt
⅛	teaspoon fresh-ground black pepper

1. In a large pot, heat the oil over moderately high heat. Add the sausage; cook, turning, until browned, about 10 minutes. Remove. Pour off all but 2 tablespoons fat.

2. Reduce the heat to moderately low. Add the onion and cook, stirring occasionally, until translucent, about 5 minutes. Add the garlic and paprika and cook, stirring, for 30 seconds longer. Remove from the heat. Cut the sausage into ½-inch slices and stir them and the tomato paste into the pot.

3. In a medium stainless-steel saucepan, combine the clam juice, wine, bay leaves, and red-pepper flakes. Discard any clams that are broken or do not clamp shut when tapped. Add the clams to the pan. Cover and bring to a boil. Cook, shaking the pan occasionally, until the clams open, about 3 minutes. Remove the open clams and continue to cook, uncovering the pan as necessary to remove the clams as soon as they open. Discard any that do not open.

4. Carefully pour the clam-cooking liquid into the sausage mixture, leaving any grit in the bottom of the pan. Add 2 tablespoons of the parsley, salt if needed, and the black pepper. Bring to a simmer, cover, and continue simmering for 5 minutes. Stir in the clams in their shells. Simmer, covered, just until the clams are warm through, about 1 minute. Serve topped with the remaining parsley.

SHRIMP-AND-FETA STEW

Shrimp and feta cheese may seem an unlikely combination, but this stew is actually a traditional Greek dish—and a delicious one. The shrimp simmer briefly in wine with tomatoes, onion, garlic, and oregano, and the cheese goes in at the last moment so that it just barely melts.

WINE RECOMMENDATION
An acidic, assertive wine such as sauvignon blanc is a natural with the feta and shrimp. Look for a bottle from New Zealand or from California.

SERVES 4

¼ cup olive oil

1 onion, chopped

2 cloves garlic, minced

3 cups diced tomatoes with their liquid (two 14½-ounce cans)

⅔ cup dry white wine

1 teaspoon dried oregano

1½ teaspoons salt

1¾ pounds large shrimp, shelled

¼ teaspoon fresh-ground black pepper

¼ pound feta cheese, cut into ¼-inch cubes

4 tablespoons chopped flat-leaf parsley

1. In a large saucepan, heat the oil over moderately low heat. Add the onion and cook, stirring occasionally, until translucent, about 5 minutes. Add the garlic and cook, stirring, 30 seconds longer.

2. Raise the heat to moderate and add the tomatoes with their liquid, the wine, oregano, and salt. Bring to a boil and cook over moderate heat, partially covered, stirring occasionally, until thickened, about 20 minutes.

3. Add the shrimp and pepper and bring back to a simmer. Simmer, covered, until the shrimp are just done, about 2 minutes. Stir in the cheese and 3 tablespoons of the parsley. Serve topped with the remaining 1 tablespoon parsley.

CHAPTER TWO

Roasted

&

Baked

WHOLE ROASTED SNAPPER WITH PARSLEY VINAIGRETTE

Cooking a fish whole keeps the flesh especially moist and flavorful—not to mention the drama an entire fish provides at serving time. Best of all, it couldn't be easier.

WINE RECOMMENDATION
The lemon and mustard in the vinaigrette will work well with an acidic white wine that doesn't have a strong flavor. Try a pinot grigio or Soave from Italy.

SERVES 4

- 1   3½-pound whole red snapper, cleaned and scaled
- 8   tablespoons olive oil
- 2   cloves garlic, minced
- 1   teaspoon salt
- 1   tablespoon plus 2 teaspoons lemon juice
- 2   large sprigs rosemary (optional)
- 2   tablespoons wine vinegar
- ½   teaspoon Dijon mustard
- ¼   teaspoon fresh-ground black pepper
- ⅓   cup chopped flat-leaf parsley

1. Heat the oven to 450°. Rinse the fish and dry the surface and the cavity thoroughly with paper towels. Put the fish on a baking sheet and cut shallow incisions about 1 inch apart in each side. Rub the fish all over with 1 tablespoon of the oil. Sprinkle both sides with the garlic, ½ teaspoon of the salt, and the 2 teaspoons lemon juice. Put the rosemary, if using, in the fish cavity. Roast the fish until just done, about 25 minutes.

2. Meanwhile, in a small glass or stainless-steel bowl, whisk together the 1 tablespoon lemon juice, the wine vinegar, the mustard, the remaining ½ teaspoon salt, and the pepper. Add the remaining 7 tablespoons oil slowly, whisking. Whisk in the parsley.

3. Serve the fish on a platter. Run a knife between the flesh and the bones and lift off the fillet with the skin attached. Turn the fish over and repeat. Pass the parsley vinaigrette.

FISH ALTERNATIVES

You can use other medium whole fish with moderately firm white flesh, such as sea bass, blackfish, grouper, or tilefish, in place of the snapper.

ORANGE AND FENNEL ROASTED COD

Fennel lovers get a triple treat with these cod fillets: The fish is anointed with a fennel-seed marinade, roasted on a bed of fennel bulbs, and then sprinkled with chopped fennel fronds before serving.

WINE RECOMMENDATION

Fennel is particularly nice when paired with a full-flavored acidic white such as a chenin blanc or sauvignon blanc. Look for a Vouvray (made from chenin blanc) or Sancerre (made from sauvignon blanc), both produced in the Loire Valley in France.

SERVES 4

- 2 fennel bulbs (about 1 pound each), including the fronds (see box)
- 1 tablespoon cooking oil
- 1 teaspoon salt
- ½ teaspoon fresh-ground black pepper
- ¼ cup fresh orange juice
- 1 teaspoon grated orange zest
- ¼ teaspoon fennel seeds
- 2 pounds cod fillets, cut to make 4 pieces

1. Heat the oven to 450°. Cut off the tops of the fennel bulbs and chop the leafy fronds. Cut each bulb into 8 wedges. In a large roasting pan, toss the fennel wedges with the oil and ¼ teaspoon each of the salt and pepper. Spread the fennel in an even layer and roast for 25 minutes. Stir the fennel and rotate the pan so the vegetables cook evenly. Roast 15 minutes longer.

2. Meanwhile, in a glass or stainless-steel bowl, combine the orange juice, orange zest, fennel seeds, and the remaining ¾ teaspoon salt and ¼ teaspoon pepper. Add the cod and marinate while the fennel roasts.

3. Remove the pan from the oven and top the fennel with the cod and its marinade. Roast until the cod is just done, about 10 minutes for ¾-inch-thick fillets. Sprinkle the chopped fennel fronds over the cod.

FISH ALTERNATIVES

Use other relatively thick, white-fleshed fillets in place of the cod. Try haddock, sea bass, or orange roughy.

FENNEL FRONDS

The wispy leaves on the top of fennel bulbs have a mild anise flavor and can be used like an herb. Some grocers cut this part off, but if you can find fennel with the fronds still attached, they're a bonus. If not, the dish will taste just fine without them.

GARLIC ROASTED COD
WITH MASHED-POTATO CRUST

Bread crumbs, cornmeal, batters of all sorts—it's not surprising to find a crust on a fish, but this one's a bit unusual. Buttery, creamy mashed potatoes are spread on fillets, which are roasted and then broiled until the topping is a tempting golden brown.

WINE RECOMMENDATION
This comforting dish will find its ideal wine soul mate in just about any chardonnay. Try a bottle from California or a more refined version—a Rully, Montagny, or Mâcon-Villages, for example—from southern Burgundy in France.

SERVES 4

2 pounds baking potatoes (about 4), peeled and cut into chunks

1¼ teaspoons salt

½ teaspoon fresh-ground black pepper

4 tablespoons butter, at room temperature

½ cup heavy cream, light cream, or milk

2 pounds cod fillets, cut to make 4 pieces

2 teaspoons cooking oil

4 cloves garlic, minced

1. Heat the oven to 450°. Put the potatoes in a medium saucepan of salted water. Bring to a boil and continue boiling until tender, about 15 minutes.

2. Drain the potatoes and put them back into the saucepan along with ¾ teaspoon of the salt and ¼ teaspoon of the pepper. Mash the potatoes over very low heat, gradually incorporating the butter and cream.

3. Rub the cod with the oil and sprinkle with the remaining ½ teaspoon salt and ¼ teaspoon pepper. Put the cod in a large roasting pan, sprinkle the fillets with the garlic, and then spread with the mashed potatoes. Roast until the fish is nearly done, 8 to 10 minutes for ¾-inch-thick fillets.

4. Heat the broiler. Broil the fish until the mashed potatoes have a golden brown crust, about 2 minutes.

FISH ALTERNATIVES

Use other relatively thick, white-fleshed fillets in place of the cod. Good choices include grouper, haddock, orange roughy, red snapper, and turbot.

PAN-ROASTED MONKFISH WITH MUSHROOMS AND SCALLIONS

The firm texture of monkfish may remind you of lobster, but with no shell to deal with, monkfish is a lot easier to eat. Here, the fillets are roasted and then topped with a creamy scallion-studded sauce.

WINE RECOMMENDATION

The meaty textures of the monkfish and mushrooms will be well served by a full-bodied chardonnay from California or Australia. The dish would even go nicely with a light red wine such as a pinot noir from California.

SERVES 4

- 1 tablespoon cooking oil
- 1 pound mushrooms, quartered if large
- 4 scallions, bulbs and green tops cut into 1-inch pieces separately
- 3 cloves garlic, chopped
- ½ teaspoon salt
- ½ teaspoon fresh-ground black pepper
- 2 pounds monkfish fillets, membranes removed, fish cut to make 4 pieces
- ¼ cup heavy cream

1. Heat the oven to 450°. In an ovenproof pot, heat the oil over moderately high heat. Add the mushrooms and cook until starting to brown, about 3 minutes. Add the scallion bulbs, garlic, and ¼ teaspoon each of the salt and pepper. Cook until the scallions start to soften, about 4 minutes.

2. Sprinkle the fish with the remaining ¼ teaspoon each salt and pepper. Put the fish on top of the mushrooms and scallions and transfer the pot to the oven. Roast until the fish is just done, 10 minutes for ¾-inch-thick fillets. Remove the monkfish from the pot and put the pot on top of the stove. Add the scallion tops and the cream to the pot. Bring to a simmer and continue simmering the sauce until it starts to thicken, 1 to 2 minutes. Serve the fish topped with the sauce.

FISH ALTERNATIVES

Thick fish steaks such as halibut or salmon would hold up well to the pan-roasting and taste delicious with this sauce.

VARIATION

PAN-ROASTED MONKFISH WITH WILD MUSHROOMS AND SCALLIONS

Use 1 pound sliced shiitake mushroom caps or 1 pound of mixed wild mushrooms in place of the regular mushrooms.

GROUPER WITH ROASTED CORN AND PEPPERS

Toss the corn and peppers with a little oil and thyme and let them roast for a few minutes before adding the fish. In no time at all, you will have a delicious dinner with only one pan to wash.

WINE RECOMMENDATION

Any number of light white wines will go nicely with this. Try a chardonnay from France, such as a Mâcon-Villages or one of the newer-styled chardonnays from the Pays d'Oc region.

SERVES 4

- 1 red bell pepper, cut into 1/2-inch squares
- 1 green bell pepper, cut into 1/2-inch squares
- 2 cups fresh (cut from about 3 ears) or frozen corn kernels
- 2 tablespoons cooking oil
- 1/2 teaspoon salt
- 1/2 teaspoon fresh-ground black pepper
- 1/2 teaspoon dried thyme
- 2 pounds grouper fillets, cut to make 4 pieces

1. Heat the oven to 450°. In a large roasting pan, combine the red and green bell peppers, the corn, 1 tablespoon of the oil, and 1/4 teaspoon each of the salt, pepper, and thyme. Roast in the oven until the corn and peppers start to brown, about 12 minutes, stirring twice.

2. Rub the remaining tablespoon oil over both sides of the fish. Sprinkle the fish with the remaining 1/4 teaspoon each salt, pepper, and thyme. Remove the roasting pan from the oven and push the corn-and-pepper mixture to the sides of the pan. Put the fish in the center of the pan, skin-side down, and cook until just done, about 15 minutes for 1-inch-thick fillets. Serve the fish with the corn and peppers.

FISH ALTERNATIVES

Other moderately firm fish to roast here include tilefish, sea bass, and cod. If the fillets are skinned, coat them with a bit of oil before adding to the pan.

TEST-KITCHEN TIP

If using frozen corn kernels, let them defrost if you can; it only takes a few minutes. Measure the corn first thing and it will be defrosted by the time you're ready for it. Pat the corn dry with a paper towel after defrosting so that the excess moisture won't get in the way during cooking and make browning impossible.

SALMON WITH RED-WINE SAUCE

The success of this simple recipe lies in the quality of the wine. Choose a full-bodied red and you'll be rewarded with a richly colored, flavorful sauce.

WINE RECOMMENDATION
Pinot noir is a classic wine match with salmon. Look for a recent vintage from either California or Oregon and chill it for fifteen minutes before serving.

SERVES 4

1 tablespoon cooking oil

4 salmon steaks, about 1 inch thick (about 2 pounds in all)

Salt

Fresh-ground black pepper

½ cup red wine

2 scallions, bulbs and green tops chopped separately

3 tablespoons butter, cut into pieces

1. Heat the oven to 450°. Put the oil in a small stainless-steel, enameled, or nonstick roasting pan and heat in the oven for 5 minutes. Season the fish with ½ teaspoon salt and ¼ teaspoon pepper. Put the fish in the hot pan; cook in the oven until just done, about 8 minutes.

2. Remove the fish from the pan and transfer to paper towels to drain. Pour off any oil remaining in the pan. Put the pan over moderate heat and add the wine and the chopped scallion bulbs. Bring to a boil, scraping the bottom of the pan to dislodge any brown bits. Cook until the wine is reduced to approximately 3 tablespoons, 1 to 2 minutes.

3. Reduce the heat to low and whisk in the butter. Season the sauce with a pinch each of salt and pepper. Put the fish on plates, browned-side up. Sprinkle the scallion greens over the top. Spoon the sauce around the fish.

FISH ALTERNATIVES

Firm tuna steaks would taste delicious with the red-wine sauce. Milder fish steaks to use include halibut and cod.

VARIATION

SALMON WITH HORSERADISH CREAM SAUCE

Roast the fish as described in step 1 but serve the roasted salmon with the horseradish cream from Crab Cakes with Horseradish Cream, page 111 (step 1), instead of with the red-wine sauce.

ROASTED SALMON WITH LENTILS AND BACON

A center-cut salmon fillet is best for roasting because it is uniform in shape and thickness and cooks more evenly than an end piece. Served on a bed of lentils that have been simmered with vegetables and bits of bacon, it's to die for.

WINE RECOMMENDATION

Light, acidic red wines are delightful with salmon, and the lentils and bacon only make the case for red wine stronger. Try a bottle of pinot noir from Oregon or California.

SERVES 4

- 4 strips bacon, cut crosswise into ½-inch pieces
- 1 small onion, cut into ½-inch slices
- 1 carrot, cut into ½-inch slices
- 1 rib celery, cut into ½-inch slices
- 1 clove garlic, minced
- 1¼ cups lentils
- 2¼ cups canned low-sodium chicken broth or homemade stock
- ½ cup canned crushed tomatoes in thick puree
- 1 teaspoon salt
- ¼ teaspoon dried thyme
- 1 bay leaf
- ¼ teaspoon fresh-ground black pepper
- 1¾ pounds skinless center-cut salmon fillet, cut into 4 pieces
- 1 tablespoon cooking oil, more if needed

1. In a medium saucepan, cook the bacon until browned. Pour off and reserve all but 2 tablespoons of the fat from the pan. Add the onion, carrot, celery, and garlic. Cook over moderate heat, stirring frequently, until golden, about 5 minutes.

2. Add the lentils, broth, tomatoes, ½ teaspoon of the salt, the thyme, and bay leaf. Bring to a boil, reduce the heat, and simmer, covered, until the lentils are just tender, about 30 minutes. Discard the bay leaf and stir in ⅛ teaspoon of the pepper.

3. Heat the oven to 450°. Sprinkle the salmon with the remaining ½ teaspoon salt and ⅛ teaspoon pepper. In a large ovenproof nonstick frying pan, over moderately high heat, heat the reserved bacon fat, with enough oil to measure 2 tablespoons. Add the fish, skinned-side up, and cook until golden, about 2 minutes. Turn. Put the pan in the oven and continue cooking the salmon until just barely done (the fish should still be translucent in the center), about 3 minutes longer for a 1-inch-thick fillet. Put the lentils on plates and top with the salmon.

ORANGE ROUGHY WITH GREMOLADA BREAD CRUMBS

Breaded fish never crisps well in the oven. Here the bread-crumb topping is prepared on the stovetop and sprinkled over the fish when it's already on the plate. Be sure to spoon the pan juices around, and not over, the fish so the crumbs stay crunchy.

WINE RECOMMENDATION
One of the new, clean-as-a-whistle white wines from Spain or the south of France will pair nicely with the Mediterranean flavors of garlic and olive oil. Look for the Spanish albariño or a Côtes de Gascogne from France.

SERVES 4

- 2 pounds orange-roughy fillets, cut to make 4 pieces
- Salt
- Fresh-ground black pepper
- ¼ cup dry white wine
- ¼ cup plus 2 tablespoons olive oil
- ½ cup dry bread crumbs
- 2 cloves garlic, minced
- Grated zest of 1 lemon
- 2 tablespoons chopped fresh parsley

1. Heat the oven to 400°. Season the orange-roughy fillets with ¼ teaspoon of salt and ⅛ teaspoon of pepper. Put the fish fillets in a glass or stainless-steel baking dish and add the wine and the ¼ cup oil to the dish. Bake the fish until just done, about 12 minutes for ¾-inch-thick fillets.

2. Meanwhile, in a small frying pan, toast the bread crumbs over low heat, stirring, until they're light brown and fragrant, about 4 minutes. Stir in the garlic, lemon zest, and parsley and cook 1 minute longer. Remove from the heat and stir in ⅛ teaspoon each salt and pepper and the remaining 2 tablespoons oil.

3. Transfer the fish to plates. Sprinkle with the bread crumbs and spoon the pan juices around the fish.

FISH ALTERNATIVES

Any mild, white-fleshed fish will work equally well here. Try flounder, sole, pike, or catfish fillets.

VARIATION

ORANGE ROUGHY WITH ORANGE GREMOLADA BREAD CRUMBS

Substitute the grated zest of ½ orange for the lemon zest in the bread-crumb mixture.

SEA BASS BAKED IN FOIL WITH PESTO, ZUCCHINI, AND CARROTS

Aluminum foil is an easy and always-available alternative to the parchment paper traditionally used for cooking *en papillote*. As the fish and vegetables bake in their packets, they render a delicious broth that is then poured over the fish at serving time.

WINE RECOMMENDATION

The assertive flavors and acidity of a sauvignon blanc will work particularly well with the pesto here. Choose one from the Alto Adige region of Italy, or try a more aggressive version from New Zealand.

SERVES 4

- 4 sea-bass fillets, about 1 inch thick (about 2 pounds in all)
- ¾ teaspoon salt
- ½ teaspoon fresh-ground black pepper
- ¼ cup pesto, store-bought or homemade
- 3 carrots, grated
- 1 zucchini, grated
- 2 tablespoons olive oil
- ¼ cup dry white wine

1. Heat the oven to 450°. Put four 12-inch squares of aluminum foil on a work surface and brush lightly with cooking oil.

2. Put a fish fillet in the center of each square of foil. Sprinkle the fillets with ¼ teaspoon of the salt and ¼ teaspoon of the pepper. Spread the fish with the pesto. Cover the pesto with the carrots and top with the zucchini. Sprinkle with the remaining ½ teaspoon salt and ¼ teaspoon pepper. Gather the foil around the fish and drizzle the fish with the oil and wine. Fold the edges of the foil to make a sealed package. Put the foil packages on a baking sheet.

3. Bake the fish until just done, about 12 minutes. Open the foil packages and transfer the fillets with their vegetable topping to plates. Pour the juices over the top.

FISH ALTERNATIVES

You can use other small, flat, white fish fillets, with or without the skin, such as red snapper, pompano, or striped bass.

SHRIMP WITH SUN-DRIED-TOMATO BARBECUE SAUCE

With jalapeños, ginger, chili powder, and an unusually large amount of black pepper in the mix, this is one spicy dish. It's based on New Orleans-style barbecued shrimp, with the added innovation of sun-dried tomatoes to thicken the irresistible, buttery sauce. Serve with plenty of crusty bread to sop it up.

WINE RECOMMENDATION
The spicy heat of the jalapeños and barbecue sauce make a beer the ideal thirst quencher for this dish. Anything but the most innocuous of wines (such as a Frascati from Italy) will be wasted here.

SERVES 4

½ cup dry-packed sun-dried tomatoes
½ cup boiling water
3 tablespoons Worcestershire sauce
4 teaspoons lemon juice
1 teaspoon salt
2 tablespoons cooking oil
3 cloves garlic, minced
2 jalapeño peppers, seeds and ribs removed, minced
1 teaspoon minced fresh ginger
2 teaspoons chili powder
1¼ teaspoons fresh-ground black pepper
¼ pound butter
2 pounds large shrimp, shelled but tails left on

1. Heat the oven to 425°. In a small bowl, combine the sun-dried tomatoes and boiling water. Let sit for 20 minutes.

2. Put the sun-dried tomatoes and their soaking liquid in a blender. Add the Worcestershire sauce, lemon juice, and salt and blend to a coarse puree.

3. In a medium saucepan, heat the oil over low heat. Add the garlic, jalapeños, and ginger and cook, stirring, for 3 minutes. Add the chili powder and black pepper and cook, stirring, for 30 seconds longer. Add the butter and melt. Remove the pan from the heat and stir in the tomato mixture. Add the shrimp and stir to combine. Put the shrimp and sauce in a 9-by-13-inch baking dish in an even layer. Bake the shrimp until just done, about 11 minutes.

Grilled
&
Broiled

TUSCAN GRILLED TROUT

A simple garlic-and-herb-infused oil combined with wine vinegar acts as both a basting liquid and a sauce for the fish. The trout skin protects the flesh and turns an appealing golden brown during grilling.

WINE RECOMMENDATION
Look for a young white wine from Italy with plenty of acidity, such as a pinot grigio or Soave, to complement the trout and stand up to the vinegar here.

SERVES 4

¼ cup olive oil

1 clove garlic, cut into thin slices

½ teaspoon dried sage

½ teaspoon dried rosemary, crumbled

2 tablespoons wine vinegar

½ teaspoon salt

¼ teaspoon fresh-ground black pepper

8 trout fillets (about 2 pounds in all)

1. Light the grill or heat the broiler. In a small stainless-steel saucepan, combine the oil, garlic, sage, and rosemary. Cook over moderately low heat until the garlic just starts to brown, about 2 minutes. Remove from the heat and immediately stir in the vinegar, ¼ teaspoon of the salt, and the pepper.

2. Put the trout fillets in a medium glass dish or stainless-steel pan. Sprinkle the fish with the remaining ¼ teaspoon salt. Add half of the oil-and-vinegar mixture and turn to coat. Grill or broil the fish skin-side down for 2 minutes. Turn and cook until just done, about 2 minutes longer for ¼-inch-thick fillets. To serve, whisk the remaining oil-and-vinegar mixture and pour it over the hot fish.

FISH ALTERNATIVES

In place of the trout, try relatively firm fillets, such as Arctic char or salmon. Whole fresh sardines, if you can find them, would also be delicious.

TEST-KITCHEN TIP

If you don't plan to grill the trout right away, let the oil and vinegar cool completely before adding the mixture to the fish. Otherwise, the hot oil and vinegar will start to cook the fish immediately.

RED SNAPPER IN GRAPE LEAVES WITH GARLIC-AND-CAPER BUTTER

Boneless fish fillets wrapped in grape leaves form neat little packages that are great for grilling or broiling. The leaves may char a bit, but don't worry; they'll taste delicious.

WINE RECOMMENDATION

The aggressive flavors and acidity of sauvignon blanc are ideal with the taste of the grape leaves and the acidity of the lemon and capers. Try a bottle from the north of Italy.

SERVES 4

- 2 pounds red-snapper fillets, skinned, cut to make 8 pieces
  Salt
  Fresh-ground black pepper
- 16 large bottled grape leaves, drained, rinsed, and dried
- 2 tablespoons cooking oil
- 4 tablespoons butter
- 2 cloves garlic, minced
  Grated zest of 1 lemon
- 1 tablespoon capers, drained
- 1 teaspoon lemon juice
- 1 tablespoon chopped fresh parsley

1. Light the grill or heat the broiler. Sprinkle the fish with ½ teaspoon salt and ¼ teaspoon pepper. Overlap two of the grape leaves and put a piece of the fish in the center. Fold the bottom of the leaves over the center of the fish. Fold in the sides of the leaves like an envelope to enclose the fish. Fold the top of the leaves over so that the fish is completely covered by the grape leaves. Brush some of the oil over the packet to seal the leaves and keep them from sticking to the grill. Repeat with the remaining fish, grape leaves, and oil, making eight packets in all.

2. Grill or broil the fish packets, turning once, until just done, about 8 minutes in all for ¾-inch-thick fillets.

3. Meanwhile, melt the butter in a small saucepan. Stir in the garlic, lemon zest, capers, lemon juice, parsley, and ⅛ teaspoon each salt and pepper. To serve, spoon the sauce over the grape-leaf packets.

FISH ALTERNATIVES

Other lean, white fish fillets, such as rockfish, haddock, pompano, or striped bass, can be substituted here, but be sure to remove the skin.

GRILLED HALIBUT WITH ORANGE RÉMOULADE

The only part of this simple supper that requires any effort is the rémoulade sauce—and that just calls for a little chopping and stirring. Dried tarragon works surprisingly well here, but use fresh, of course, if you have it on hand.

WINE RECOMMENDATION

The capers, mustard, and orange juice will go very well with a light, lively white wine with plenty of acidity. Try a pinot grigio from Italy, preferably from the northern Alto Adige region.

SERVES 4

¾ cup mayonnaise

2 tablespoons Dijon mustard

4 teaspoons fresh orange juice

¼ teaspoon dried tarragon, or ¾ teaspoon chopped fresh tarragon

2 teaspoons drained capers, chopped

2 dilled gherkins, chopped

½ teaspoon anchovy paste

1 tablespoon chopped fresh parsley

Fresh-ground black pepper

4 halibut steaks, about 1 inch thick (about 2 pounds in all)

1 tablespoon cooking oil

½ teaspoon salt

1. In a small glass or stainless-steel bowl, whisk together the mayonnaise, mustard, orange juice, tarragon, capers, gherkins, anchovy paste, parsley, and ⅛ teaspoon pepper.

2. Light the grill or heat the broiler. Coat the halibut with the oil and season with the salt and ¼ teaspoon pepper. Grill or broil the fish for 3 minutes. Turn and cook until just done, about 4 minutes longer. Serve the fish with the orange rémoulade.

FISH ALTERNATIVES

Serve grilled or broiled salmon steaks, salmon fillets, or skewered sea scallops with the rémoulade in place of the halibut.

MAHIMAHI WITH SAGE GARLIC CHIPS

Thin slices of garlic cooked in olive oil make a double contribution to this dish: The flavorful oil is used for basting the fish, and the garlic "chips" are sprinkled over the finished dish as a crunchy topping.

WINE RECOMMENDATION
Garlic invites refreshing sips between bites but can overwhelm many wines. Try an easy-drinking rosé or a white zinfandel from California.

SERVES 4

½ cup olive oil

12 cloves garlic, cut into thin slices

1 tablespoon dried sage

¾ teaspoon salt

½ teaspoon fresh-ground black pepper

4 mahimahi steaks, about ¾ inch thick (about 2 pounds in all)

1. In a small saucepan, combine the oil, garlic, sage, and ¼ teaspoon each of the salt and pepper. Cook over low heat, stirring occasionally, until the garlic just starts to brown, 8 to 10 minutes. Don't let it brown thoroughly, or it will taste bitter. Strain the oil into a small bowl, reserving the cooked garlic.

2. Light the grill or heat the broiler. Brush some of the oil over the fish and then season with the remaining ½ teaspoon salt and ¼ teaspoon pepper. Grill or broil the fish, basting with the oil, for 4 minutes. Turn and cook, basting with the oil, until just done, 3 to 4 minutes longer. You should have about 2 tablespoons of the flavored oil remaining.

3. To serve, drizzle the remaining oil over the fish. Top with the cooked garlic.

FISH ALTERNATIVES

Try another firm fish, such as mako shark, swordfish, or tuna steaks.

VARIATIONS

MAHIMAHI WITH THYME GARLIC CHIPS

Use 1 tablespoon dried thyme in place of the sage.

MAHIMAHI WITH OREGANO GARLIC CHIPS

Use 1 tablespoon dried oregano in place of the sage.

GRILLED SWORDFISH WITH TOMATO-AND-CUCUMBER SALSA

Cooking fish on an outdoor grill is one of the joys of summer. Firm swordfish steaks are particularly well suited to this method, and here we've topped them with a seasonal salsa of cucumber, dill, and grilled tomatoes. The dish can also be made in the broiler.

WINE RECOMMENDATION
A light white wine with plenty of refreshing acidity is perfect with both the fish and the fresh vegetables. Try a Muscadet de Sèvre-et-Maine from the Loire Valley in France.

SERVES 4

1¼ pounds plum tomatoes (about 6), halved crosswise

1 tablespoon cooking oil

1 cucumber, peeled, halved lengthwise, seeded, and cut into ¼-inch dice

1½ teaspoons lemon juice or wine vinegar

1 tablespoon chopped fresh dill

1 teaspoon salt

½ teaspoon fresh-ground black pepper

4 swordfish steaks, about 1 inch thick (about 2 pounds in all)

1. Light the grill or heat the broiler. Coat the tomato halves with 1 teaspoon of the oil. Grill the tomatoes cut-side up (or broil them cut-side down), until the skins start to blacken, about 10 minutes. Slip off the skins and put the tomatoes in a medium glass or stainless-steel bowl. Add the cucumber, lemon juice, dill,

¾ teaspoon of the salt, and ¼ teaspoon of the pepper. Stir to break up the tomatoes and to combine the ingredients.

2. Coat the swordfish with the remaining 2 teaspoons oil and sprinkle with the remaining ¼ teaspoon salt and ¼ teaspoon pepper. Grill or broil the fish for 4 minutes. Turn and cook until golden brown and just done, 4 to 5 minutes longer. Serve with the salsa.

FISH ALTERNATIVES

Halibut, marlin, and salmon steaks are also delicious grilled, and any of these would go well with the salsa.

VARIATIONS

Use 1 tablespoon chopped fresh basil in place of the dill. A tablespoon of fresh mint is another tasty alternative.

GRILLED SWORDFISH WITH CHARMOULA

Charmoula is a flavorful Moroccan tomato sauce flavored with cumin, lemon, and plenty of cilantro or parsley, and it couldn't be easier to make. Just throw the ingredients in a blender or food processor and puree.

WINE RECOMMENDATION
Choose a pinot blanc from Alsace in France or a pinot gris from Oregon; both are delightful, easy-drinking white wines that will have enough body and the requisite moderate acidity to pair with the spicy tomato sauce.

SERVES 4

¾   cup canned crushed tomatoes in thick puree

5   tablespoons olive oil

3½ teaspoons lemon juice

1½ teaspoons ground cumin

1½ teaspoons paprika

½   teaspoon dried oregano

¼   teaspoon ground ginger

1   teaspoon salt

¼   teaspoon fresh-ground black pepper

⅓   cup chopped flat-leaf parsley

4   swordfish steaks, about 1 inch thick (about 2 pounds in all)

1. Light the grill or heat the broiler. Put the tomatoes in a blender or food processor and add 4 tablespoons of the oil, the lemon juice, cumin, paprika, oregano, ginger, ¾ teaspoon of the salt, ⅛ teaspoon of the pepper, and the parsley. Blend just until the mixture becomes a coarse puree.

2. Coat the swordfish with the remaining 1 tablespoon oil and sprinkle with the remaining ¼ teaspoon salt and ⅛ teaspoon pepper. Grill or broil the fish for 4 minutes. Turn and cook until golden brown and just done, about 4 minutes longer. Serve the sauce alongside.

FISH ALTERNATIVES

Cod, halibut, tilefish, mahimahi, mako shark, sturgeon, tuna—just about any fish steaks can stand in for the swordfish.

GRILLED TUNA WITH MINT SAUCE

Fresh mint blends with garlic, vinegar, and sugar for a room-temperature sweet-and-sour sauce that's traditional in England with roasted lamb—and is also perfect for a full-flavored fish like tuna. Serve the rather forceful sauce separately so that each person can decide how much or little to use.

WINE RECOMMENDATION
Look for the lightest, leanest white you can find; anything else will have a tough time with the mint. Try a verdicchio-based wine from Italy or a vinho verde from Portugal.

SERVES 4

- ½ cup chopped fresh mint
- 3 tablespoons water
- 2 tablespoons sugar
- ½ cup white-wine vinegar
- 2 cloves garlic, minced
- ¾ teaspoon salt
- 4 tuna steaks, about 1 inch thick (about 2 pounds in all)
- 1 tablespoon olive oil
- ¼ teaspoon fresh-ground black pepper

1. Put ⅓ cup of the mint in a medium glass or stainless-steel bowl. In a small stainless-steel saucepan, bring the water to a simmer over moderate heat. Add the sugar and stir until completely dissolved. Stir in the vinegar, garlic, and ¼ teaspoon of the salt. Pour the mixture over the mint in the bowl. Let sit 15 minutes.

2. Light the grill or heat the broiler. Coat the tuna with the oil. Season with the remaining ½ teaspoon salt and the pepper. Cook the tuna for 4 minutes. Turn and cook until done to your taste, 3 to 4 minutes longer for medium rare.

3. Strain the mint sauce through a sieve into a sauceboat or serving bowl. Stir in the remaining mint. Pass the sauce with the fish.

FISH ALTERNATIVES

Mackerel and salmon are both full-flavored enough to take on this sauce.

GRILLED TUNA WITH LEMON ANCHOVY BUTTER

Few meals are quicker to put together than this—grilled fish steaks topped with a simple compound butter. For even faster preparation, make the butter ahead of time and store it in the freezer until ready to use. The anchovy flavor here is quite mild; add more anchovy paste to suit your taste.

WINE RECOMMENDATION
The trick here is to find a wine with enough body to go with the tuna but lots of acidity to stand up to the flavorful lemon anchovy butter. Try a sauvignon blanc from New Zealand or from California.

SERVES 4

- 4 tablespoons butter, at room temperature
- ½ teaspoon anchovy paste
- 1 teaspoon lemon juice
- 1 tablespoon chopped fresh parsley
  Salt
  Fresh-ground black pepper
- 4 tuna steaks, about 1 inch thick (about 2 pounds in all)
- 1 tablespoon cooking oil

1. Light the grill or heat the broiler. In a small bowl, combine the butter, anchovy paste, lemon juice, parsley, and a pinch each of salt and pepper.

2. Coat the tuna with the oil. Sprinkle with ½ teaspoon salt and ¼ teaspoon pepper. Cook the tuna for 4 minutes. Turn and cook until done to your taste, 3 to 4 minutes longer for medium rare. Top the hot fish with the flavored butter.

FISH ALTERNATIVES

The lemon anchovy butter would also be very good with grilled halibut, swordfish, or salmon steaks.

VARIATION

GRILLED TUNA WITH SUN-DRIED-TOMATO BASIL BUTTER

Mix 1 tablespoon chopped fresh basil, 3 chopped oil-packed or reconstituted sun-dried tomatoes, and a pinch each of salt and pepper into 4 tablespoons room-temperature butter. Use this mixture in place of the lemon anchovy butter.

FRESH SARDINES ON GRILLED BREAD

Grilled the Portuguese way with olive oil and coarse salt, these sardines are delectable. They're served on thick slices of toasted country bread that soften slightly and gain flavor as the sardine juices soak in. You'll be surprised how easy it is to fillet the sardines at the table; the meat virtually separates itself from the spine and bones.

WINE RECOMMENDATION
The saltiness of the sardines and the rusticity of this dish are perfect with a very cold bottle of unassuming and refreshing vinho verde from Portugal. Many vinho verdes are nonvintage, but if those available to you are dated, choose as young a bottle as possible.

SERVES 4

4   ³⁄₄-inch-thick slices bread, from a large country loaf

6   tablespoons olive oil

¹⁄₄   teaspoon table salt

16   large sardines, cleaned (about 2 pounds in all)

1   tablespoon coarse salt

1. Light the grill or heat the broiler. Using 4¹⁄₂ tablespoons of the oil, brush both sides of each slice of bread. Sprinkle both sides with the table salt. Grill or broil the bread, turning once, until crisp and golden on the surface but still soft inside, about 4 minutes in all.

2. Rub the sardines all over with the remaining 1¹⁄₂ tablespoons oil and sprinkle with the coarse salt. Grill or broil the sardines for 4 minutes. Turn and cook until golden brown and just done, about 3 minutes. To serve, top each piece of grilled bread with 4 sardines.

FISH ALTERNATIVES

Sweeter than sardines, smelts are an ideal alternative here. They're usually smaller, so cook them a little less.

SEAFOOD MIXED GRILL WITH RED-PEPPER SAUCE

There's no law that says a mixed grill has to be based on meat. Shrimp, scallops, and salmon are up to the task, and, paired with a simple red-pepper sauce, make for a festive meal. Add bread, salad, and wine and you have a party.

WINE RECOMMENDATION
A full-bodied, expansive wine such as a California chardonnay is ideal with the meaty, flavorful shrimp, scallops, and salmon. For the roasted red peppers and garlic, it's best to choose one that's not oaky.

SERVES 4

1   7-ounce jar roasted red peppers, drained and rinsed (about ¾ cup)

1   clove garlic

½   teaspoon wine vinegar

2   tablespoons chopped fresh parsley

½   teaspoon sugar

4   tablespoons cooking oil

¾   teaspoon salt
    Fresh-ground black pepper

½   pound medium shrimp, shelled

½   pound sea scallops

1   pound center-cut salmon fillet, cut into 4 pieces

1.   In a food processor or blender, puree the red peppers and garlic with the vinegar, parsley, sugar, 3 tablespoons of the oil, ¼ teaspoon of the salt, and ¼ teaspoon of black pepper.

2.   Light the grill or heat the broiler. Thread the shrimp on four skewers and the scallops on four skewers. Coat the shellfish with 2 teaspoons of the oil and sprinkle with ¼ teaspoon of the salt and ¼ teaspoon black pepper. Coat the salmon with the remaining 1 teaspoon oil and sprinkle with ⅛ teaspoon of black pepper and the remaining ¼ teaspoon salt.

3.   Grill or broil the fish, turning once, until just done, about 2 to 3 minutes per side for the shrimp, 3 to 4 minutes per side for the scallops, and 3 to 4 minutes per side for a 1-inch-thick salmon fillet (the fish should still be translucent in the center). Serve with the red-pepper sauce.

FISH ALTERNATIVES

Feel free to use only one or two types of the fish and shellfish listed. Other grilled fish that would be nice with the red-pepper sauce include halibut, swordfish, tuna, or mahimahi.

JERK CATFISH

The Jamaican spice treatment called *jerk* isn't just for meat and chicken; it's great on fish, too. Rub the spice paste on catfish fillets and broil for a crisp, spicy coating. Though the sesame seeds aren't traditional, they add a pleasant crunch and rich flavor.

WINE RECOMMENDATION
Make your beverage choice as simple and casual as this dish—and look for something that can take the heat. Try either a white zinfandel, a rosé, or your favorite beer.

SERVES 4

⅓ cup chopped onion

1 clove garlic, smashed

1 tablespoon sesame seeds

2 teaspoons brown sugar

1½ teaspoons ground allspice

1½ teaspoons dried thyme

½ teaspoon grated nutmeg

1¼ teaspoons salt

¼ teaspoon fresh-ground black pepper

¼ teaspoon cayenne

2½ tablespoons cooking oil

½ teaspoon vinegar

2 pounds catfish fillets

1. In a blender, puree the onion, garlic, and sesame seeds with the brown sugar, allspice, thyme, nutmeg, 1 teaspoon of the salt, the black pepper, cayenne, oil, and vinegar. Heat the broiler. Lightly oil a broiler pan or baking sheet.

2. Sprinkle both sides of the catfish fillets with the remaining ¼ teaspoon salt and put them on the prepared baking sheet, skinned-side down. Spread the spice mixture over the fish in an even layer.

3. Broil the fish, about 6 inches from the heat if possible, until well-browned and just done, about 5 minutes for ¾-inch-thick fillets.

FISH ALTERNATIVES

Though catfish is lean and firm, those qualities aren't imperative here. You can use fillets of a different nature, such as bluefish, red snapper, or wolffish.

BROILED SHAD WITH THYME

Don't be alarmed if the shad fillets are heavily cut into; shad is one of the boniest fish there is, and removing all the bones requires radical surgery. What you're left with, however, are succulent fillets that are ideal for broiling.

WINE RECOMMENDATION
The richness of this simple preparation is delightful accompanied by an acidic chardonnay. Look for a reasonably priced Mâcon-Villages or Chablis, both from Burgundy in France.

SERVES 4

2   pounds shad fillets, cut to make 4 pieces

1   tablespoon olive oil

¾   teaspoon chopped fresh thyme, plus thyme sprigs for garnish (optional), or ¼ teaspoon dried thyme

½   teaspoon salt

⅛   teaspoon fresh-ground black pepper

1   tablespoon butter

4   lemon wedges, for serving

FISH ALTERNATIVES

There's nothing quite like shad. Still, this is a good basic broiled fish recipe to use with other fish fillets, such as red snapper, sea bass, striped bass, pompano, and bluefish.

VARIATION

BROILED SHAD WITH OREGANO

Use ¾ teaspoon fresh or ¼ teaspoon dried oregano in place of the thyme.

---

1. Heat the broiler. Lightly oil a broiler pan or baking sheet. Put the fish in the pan and rub the surface with the oil. Sprinkle with the chopped or dried thyme, the salt, and pepper. Dot with the butter.

2. Broil the fish until golden brown and just done, about 4 minutes for ¾-inch-thick fillets. Decorate with the thyme sprigs, if using. Serve with the lemon wedges.

TERIYAKI SALMON

You can make the teriyaki glaze in minutes, and the whole dish takes only a little longer. Keep a sharp eye on the salmon during cooking, though; the glaze can burn if the heat's too high.

WINE RECOMMENDATION
Soy sauce is notoriously tough to pair with wine, which is one reason beer is so often served with Japanese food. A moderately priced sparkling wine from California is another possibility. This will stand up to the soy sauce and cut through the richness of the salmon.

SERVES 4

½ cup soy sauce

½ cup mirin or sweet sherry

¼ cup sugar

4 salmon steaks, about 1 inch thick (about 2 pounds in all)

1. Heat the broiler or light the grill. If broiling, line a broiler pan or baking sheet with aluminum foil and lightly oil the foil.

2. In a medium stainless-steel saucepan, bring the soy sauce, mirin, and sugar to a boil, stirring. Reduce the heat and simmer, stirring occasionally, until thickened and reduced to ⅔ cup, about 10 minutes.

3. If broiling, put the salmon in the prepared pan. Brush the salmon with the soy-sauce mixture. Broil or grill until well browned, about 2 minutes. Turn and brush with more of the soy-sauce mixture. Continue cooking until the fish is browned and just barely done (the fish should still be translucent in the center), about 3 minutes longer. Brush with the remaining soy-sauce mixture and serve.

FISH ALTERNATIVES

If you can find sablefish—a rich, succulent fish also called black cod, though it's very different from regular cod—by all means use it. Other alternatives are bluefish or mackerel fillets, but don't turn them during cooking or they may fall apart.

IN PLACE OF MIRIN

This is one case where the substitute really is just as good as the original ingredient. In fact, in our taste tests we could barely tell the difference between this recipe prepared with mirin (sweet Asian cooking wine) and with sweet sherry. You can also use six tablespoons dry sherry and add an additional three tablespoons sugar.

BROILED BLUEFISH WITH RED ONION AND CITRUS DRESSING

Acidic ingredients, like the grapefruit and lime juices in the marinade and dressing, complement oily bluefish. Broiling is an ideal method for this fish, but watch the red onion closely to make sure it doesn't burn.

WINE RECOMMENDATION

Just as the citrus here flatters the fish, a light white wine with lots of acidity will balance its oiliness while matching the grapefruit and lime flavors. Try a vinho verde from Portugal or a sauvignon blanc from South Africa.

SERVES 4

¼ cup olive oil

2 tablespoons grapefruit juice

2 tablespoons lime juice

¾ teaspoon salt

2 tablespoons chopped fresh chives or scallion tops

2 pounds bluefish fillets, cut to make 4 pieces

1 small red onion, cut into thin slices

¼ teaspoon fresh-ground black pepper

1. In a small bowl, combine the oil, grapefruit juice, lime juice, ¼ teaspoon of the salt, and 1 tablespoon of the chives.

2. Put the fish, skin-side down, in a shallow glass dish or stainless-steel pan. Scatter the onion over the fish. Pour half of the citrus dressing over the top; let marinate for about 15 minutes.

3. Heat the broiler. Put the fish, skin-side down, on a broiler pan or baking sheet. Sprinkle with the remaining ½ teaspoon salt and the pepper. Top with the onion. Broil the fish, about 6 inches from the heat if possible, until just done, about 5 minutes for ¾-inch-thick fillets.

4. Pour the remaining dressing over the hot fish and sprinkle with the remaining tablespoon of the chives.

FISH ALTERNATIVES

Any rich, full-flavored fish fillets would benefit from the acidity in the citrus dressing. Try mackerel, shad, kingfish, or porgy.

Sautéed
&
Fried

SOLE WITH LEMON CREAM

You can use any type of sole for this dish, such as Petrale, lemon, or gray. They're all delicate in flavor, as is the simple lemon cream sauce. The balance in strength ensures that neither will overwhelm the other; the sauce just enhances the fillets.

WINE RECOMMENDATION

A ripe, full-flavored chardonnay with oak overtones will be well suited to the richness of this creamy dish. Try a bottle from California or Australia.

SERVES 4

2 tablespoons butter

2 pounds sole fillets, cut to make 4 pieces

¾ teaspoon salt

¼ teaspoon fresh-ground black pepper

¼ cup flour

¾ cup heavy cream

   Grated zest of ½ lemon

1 tablespoon lemon juice

2 tablespoons chopped fresh parsley

1. In a large nonstick frying pan, melt the butter over moderate heat. Sprinkle the sole with ½ teaspoon of the salt and the pepper. Dust the sole with the flour and shake off any excess. Put the sole in the pan and cook for 2 minutes. Turn and cook until just done, about 2 minutes longer. Remove the sole from the pan.

2. Add the cream and lemon zest to the pan. Bring to a simmer and cook until starting to thicken, about 2 minutes. Stir in the remaining ¼ teaspoon salt, the lemon juice, and parsley. Serve the sauce over the fish.

FISH ALTERNATIVES

Other members of the flounder family, such as sand dab or fluke, will go well with the sauce, as will such mild fish fillets as trout, hake, or whiting.

95

CRISP LIME BROOK TROUT

The oil must be really hot when the fish hits the pan for the skin to turn crisp and golden. Shake the pan back and forth on the burner occasionally to keep the trout from sticking to the bottom and tearing the skin.

WINE RECOMMENDATION
The tart lime and crisp fish call for a white wine with good acidity. A California or New Zealand sauvignon blanc will be good here.

SERVES 4

- 1 tablespoon lime juice
- ½ teaspoon grated lime zest
- 1⅛ teaspoons salt
-    Fresh-ground black pepper
- ½ cup olive oil
- 3 tablespoons cooking oil, plus more if needed
- 8 trout fillets (about 2 pounds in all)

1. In a small bowl, whisk together the lime juice, lime zest, ⅛ teaspoon of the salt, and a pinch of pepper. Add the olive oil slowly, whisking. Heat the oven to 200°. Cover a baking sheet with paper towels.

2. In a large nonstick frying pan, heat the cooking oil over moderately high heat. Sprinkle the trout with the remaining 1 teaspoon salt and ½ teaspoon pepper. Put half the fillets in the pan, skin-side down, and cook until golden, about 3 minutes. Turn and cook until just done, about 1 minute longer. Transfer the fillets to the prepared baking sheet, skin-side up and keep warm in the oven while cooking the remaining fillets. Add more oil between batches if necessary. Serve, skin-side up, surrounded by the lime dressing.

FISH ALTERNATIVES

The acidity of the lime juice in the dressing pairs well with a wide range of fish. Try sautéed or grilled kingfish, mackerel, or porgy fillets.

VARIATION

CRISP LIME BROOK TROUT WITH FRESH HERBS

Add 2 tablespoons chopped fresh cilantro, parsley, or chives to the dressing.

SAUTÉED BROOK TROUT WITH BROWN BUTTER AND PECANS

Brown butter is a sublimely simple sauce. Emphasize the butter's nutty flavor with pecans, throw in a little sage and parsley, and you have an ideal topping for trout.

WINE RECOMMENDATION
A full, luscious white wine will accentuate the deep nutty flavors of this dish. Look for an Australian chardonnay, with its ripe fruitiness and toasty oak.

SERVES 4

- 2 tablespoons cooking oil
- 8 trout fillets (about 2 pounds in all)
- ½ teaspoon salt
- ¼ teaspoon fresh-ground black pepper
- 4 tablespoons butter
- ½ teaspoon dried sage
- ½ cup chopped pecans
- 2 tablespoons chopped fresh parsley

1. Heat the oven to 250°. Cover a baking sheet with paper towels.

2. In a large nonstick frying pan, heat 1 tablespoon of the oil over moderate heat. Sprinkle the fish with the salt and pepper. Put half the trout in the pan and cook for 2 minutes. Turn and cook until browned and just done, 1 to 2 minutes longer. Transfer the cooked fillets to the prepared baking sheet and keep warm in the oven. Add the remaining 1 tablespoon oil to the pan, cook the rest of the trout fillets, and add them to the baking sheet.

3. Wipe out the frying pan and melt the butter over low heat. Add the sage and pecans and cook, stirring, until the butter is golden brown, about 5 minutes. Stir in the parsley. Serve the trout with the butter sauce spooned over the top.

FISH ALTERNATIVES

The combination of pecans and brown butter complements many kinds of fish, such as black bass, lake perch, or walleye.

SESAME-CRUSTED SALMON

Cornstarch, egg white, and sesame seeds form a crackling crust on these salmon fillets. The flavor of the toasted sesame seeds is complemented by the Asian-flavored sauce surrounding the fish, but don't serve the sauce over the fish or you'll lose the crunch.

WINE RECOMMENDATION
Salmon is generally best with a light red or a substantial white. Pinot noir is the usual red suggested. With the Asian ingredients here, a white such as a pinot gris from Oregon or Alsace in France will make a delicious pairing.

SERVES 4

¼ cup soy sauce

2 tablespoons dry sherry

½ cup canned low-sodium chicken broth or homemade stock

½ teaspoon sugar

1½ teaspoons grated fresh ginger

1 clove garlic, minced

2 tablespoons plus 2 teaspoons cornstarch

3 tablespoons water

1 egg white

2 pounds center-cut salmon fillet, cut into 4 pieces

¼ cup sesame seeds

¼ cup cooking oil

1. In a small bowl, combine the soy sauce, sherry, chicken broth, sugar, ginger, and garlic. In another small bowl, stir together the 2 teaspoons cornstarch and the water.

2. Whisk together the egg white and the 2 tablespoons cornstarch. Brush the skinless side of the salmon with the egg-white mixture and then dip it into the sesame seeds to coat.

3. In a large nonstick frying pan, heat the oil over moderately high heat. Put the salmon in the pan, sesame-seed side down, and cook until golden brown, about 5 minutes. Turn and cook until just done, about 3 minutes longer for a 1-inch-thick fillet. Remove.

4. Pour any oil from the pan. Add the soy-sauce mixture. Simmer for 2 minutes, stirring. Whisk in the cornstarch-and-water mixture and cook, stirring, until thickened, about 1 minute longer. Serve the salmon with the sauce poured around it.

FISH ALTERNATIVES

Tuna steaks would be perfect with the sesame-seed crust and the sauce. You can also use salmon steaks instead of fillets.

KOREAN-STYLE SEARED TUNA

Soy sauce, sesame oil, scallion, garlic, dried chiles—these traditional Korean flavorings, combined with chicken stock, make an intense and delicious sauce for the tuna. Sautéed spinach or broccoli rabe tossed with a touch of soy sauce and a sprinkling of sesame seeds would be a delicious accompaniment.

WINE RECOMMENDATION

An aromatic white wine with just a touch of residual sweetness will buffer the spiciness of this dish and balance the saltiness from the soy sauce. Try a luscious sauvignon blanc from New Zealand or California.

SERVES 4

- 3 tablespoons soy sauce
- 1 teaspoon sugar
- 1/8 teaspoon dried red-pepper flakes
- 1/2 cup canned low-sodium chicken broth or homemade stock
- 4 tuna steaks, about 1 inch thick (about 2 pounds in all)
- 1/2 teaspoon salt
- 1/2 teaspoon fresh-ground black pepper
- 2 tablespoons cooking oil
- 1 teaspoon Asian sesame oil
- 1 scallion including green top, chopped
- 3 cloves garlic, minced

1. In a small bowl, combine the soy sauce, sugar, red-pepper flakes, and broth. Sprinkle the fish with the salt and black pepper. Heat the cooking oil in a large frying pan over moderately high heat. Add the tuna and cook until brown, about 3 minutes. Turn and cook the fish until done to your taste, 3 to 4 minutes longer for medium rare.

2. Reduce the heat to moderately low and put the sesame oil in the pan. Stir in the scallion and garlic and cook, stirring, for 1 minute. Add the soy-sauce mixture; simmer until reduced to approximately 1/3 cup, about 2 minutes. Cut the tuna into slices and serve with the sauce.

FISH ALTERNATIVES

Salmon fillets or steaks will also go well with this highly seasoned sauce.

TEST-KITCHEN TIP

We like fresh tuna cooked to a succulent medium rare. If you prefer your tuna cooked through, just add a few more minutes to the cooking time. Be careful not to overcook it, though, or it will most assuredly be dry.

SEARED TUNA WITH AVOCADO AND SALSA VERDE

Salsa verde is a pungent Italian sauce made with capers, parsley, and anchovies. It stands up nicely to the meaty tuna steaks, while serving as a perfect foil for the mild avocado.

WINE RECOMMENDATION

The brazen flavors of anchovy paste and capers make a white wine with lots of acidity a must. A Sancerre or a lighter-styled Muscadet de Sèvre-et-Maine, both from the Loire Valley in France, are good examples.

SERVES 4

²⁄₃ cup lightly packed flat-leaf parsley leaves

3 tablespoons drained capers

1 clove garlic, smashed

4 teaspoons lemon juice

1 teaspoon anchovy paste

½ teaspoon Dijon mustard

¾ teaspoon salt

¼ teaspoon fresh-ground black pepper

½ cup plus 1 tablespoon olive oil

4 tuna steaks, about 1 inch thick (about 2 pounds in all)

1 avocado, cut into ½-inch chunks

1. Put the parsley, capers, garlic, lemon juice, anchovy paste, mustard, ½ teaspoon of the salt, and ⅛ teaspoon of the pepper into a food processor. Pulse to chop, six to eight times. With the machine running, add the ½ cup oil in a thin stream to make a coarse puree. Leave the sauce in the food processor and, if necessary, pulse to re-emulsify just before serving.

2. Heat a grill pan or heavy cast-iron pan over moderately high heat. Rub the tuna steaks all over with the 1 tablespoon oil. Sprinkle with the remaining ¼ teaspoon salt and ⅛ teaspoon pepper. Cook the fish for 3 minutes. Turn and cook until done to your taste, 3 to 4 minutes longer for medium rare. To serve, top the tuna steaks with the avocado and drizzle with the sauce.

FISH ALTERNATIVES

Firm fish steaks, such as sturgeon, mako shark, and swordfish, all make excellent alternatives to the tuna. You'll want to cook them longer until just done, rather than medium rare.

SEARED SCALLOPS WITH ORANGE AND VERMOUTH

Be sure to dry the scallops thoroughly before cooking so they'll brown nicely. A quick pan sauce of vermouth, butter, and orange zest adds a delectable flavor.

WINE RECOMMENDATION

A light, acidic white wine is a good partner for the citrus here. Outstanding choices would be a better quality Soave or a sauvignon blanc from the northern Alto Adige region of Italy.

SERVES 4

- 2 tablespoons cooking oil
- 2 pounds sea scallops
- ½ teaspoon salt
- ⅛ teaspoon fresh-ground black pepper
- 3 tablespoons butter
- 2 scallions including green tops, chopped
- ½ cup dry vermouth
- 1 teaspoon grated orange zest

1. In a large nonstick frying pan, heat 1 tablespoon of the oil over moderately high heat until very hot. Season the scallops with the salt and pepper. Add half the scallops to the pan and cook until browned, about 1 minute. Turn and cook until browned on the second side and just done, about 2 minutes longer. Remove from the pan. Add the remaining tablespoon oil to the pan and repeat with the remaining scallops. Wipe out the pan.

2. In the same pan, melt the butter over moderate heat. Add the scallions and cook, stirring, for 1 minute. Add the vermouth and orange zest. Cook until the sauce thickens slightly, about 2 minutes. Add the scallops and warm until just heated through, about 1 minute.

FISH ALTERNATIVES

Instead of large sea scallops, you can use bay scallops. Sauté them for just a minute and a half. They cook so quickly there's not time for a brown crust to form, but the taste will still be delicious.

VARIATIONS

SEARED SCALLOPS WITH LEMON AND VERMOUTH

Use 1 teaspoon of grated lemon zest in place of the orange zest.

SEARED SCALLOPS WITH ORANGE AND WHITE WINE

Use ½ cup of dry white wine in place of the vermouth.

SOFT-SHELL CRABS IN BACON ON ARUGULA WITH MUSTARD VINAIGRETTE

Bacon becomes a crunchy crust surrounding each crab, and peppery arugula with mustard vinaigrette is the perfect counterpoint. Mark this recipe to use in the spring when both soft-shells and the first tender arugula are in season.

WINE RECOMMENDATION
The richness of the bacon will pair nicely with a full-flavored wine, but there should be some acidity to stand up to the spicy arugula and vinaigrette. The solution? A pinot blanc from Alsace, which nicely combines both of these qualities.

SERVES 4

     2 teaspoons wine vinegar
1½ teaspoons grainy or Dijon mustard
     ¾ teaspoon salt
        Fresh-ground black pepper
2½ tablespoons olive oil
     8 soft-shell crabs, cleaned
    16 slices bacon (about ¾ pound)
     ½ cup flour
     3 tablespoons cooking oil
1½ quarts arugula leaves (from about two ¼-pound bunches)

1. In a medium glass or stainless-steel bowl, whisk together the vinegar, mustard, ¼ teaspoon of the salt, and ⅛ teaspoon pepper. Add the olive oil slowly, whisking.

2. Wrap the body of each crab with two slices of bacon without overlapping, leaving the legs exposed. In a shallow bowl, combine the flour, the remaining ½ teaspoon of the salt, and ¼ teaspoon pepper.

3. In each of two large frying pans, heat 1½ tablespoons of the cooking oil over moderately high heat. Dust the crabs and bacon with the flour mixture and shake off the excess. Put the crabs in the pans, upside down. Cook until the bacon is browned and crisp, about 3 minutes. Turn and cook until the bacon on the other side is browned and crisp and the crabs are just done, about 3 minutes longer.

4. To serve, toss the arugula with the vinaigrette and mound on four plates. Top the salad with the crabs.

CRAB CAKES WITH HORSERADISH CREAM

Lump crabmeat is mixed with only enough bread crumbs and mayonnaise to hold it together, then coated with more crumbs and fried to a golden brown. A mixture of sour cream and horseradish provides lively accompaniment.

WINE RECOMMENDATION

A full-bodied white such as a chardonnay from California will be delightful with the crab. Try to find one that isn't too oaky—just full of the taste of ripe fruit.

SERVES 4

½ cup sour cream

½ cup mayonnaise

2 tablespoons drained bottled horseradish

1 pound lump crabmeat, picked free of shell

1 cup dry bread crumbs

3 scallions including green tops, chopped

¼ cup chopped fresh parsley

Pinch cayenne

¼ teaspoon salt

¼ teaspoon fresh-ground black pepper

3 tablespoons cooking oil

1. In a small bowl, whisk together the sour cream, ¼ cup of the mayonnaise, and the horseradish.

2. In a large bowl, combine the crabmeat, the remaining ¼ cup mayonnaise, ¼ cup of the bread crumbs, the scallions, parsley, cayenne, salt, and pepper. Shape the crab mixture into eight patties. Coat the patties with the remaining ¾ cup bread crumbs and pat off the excess.

3. In a large nonstick frying pan, heat the oil over moderate heat. Working in batches if necessary, fry the cakes until golden brown and crisp, about 2 minutes. Turn and fry until golden brown on the other side, about 2 minutes longer. Drain on paper towels. Serve with the horseradish cream.

FISH ALTERNATIVES

There's really no substitute for sweet fresh crabmeat—but for a completely different taste, you could use one pound of cod, cooked and flaked.

Southern Crab Hash

Chunks of crisp potato, bits of bacon, and tender morsels of crab are held together with melting cream cheese for a spectacular sort of Southern-accented comfort food.

WINE RECOMMENDATION
The sweetness of crab is often at its best paired with a full-bodied chardonnay, which will also be good with the bacon, potatoes, and cream cheese. Try a bottle from California or Australia.

SERVES 4

- 2 pounds boiling potatoes, peeled and cut into ¾-inch pieces
- 6 slices bacon
- 1 onion, chopped
  Cooking oil, if needed
- ½ teaspoon salt
- 3 ounces cream cheese
- ¼ cup milk
- 1½ teaspoons Worcestershire sauce
  Pinch cayenne
- ¾ pound lump crabmeat
- ⅛ teaspoon fresh-ground black pepper
- 3 tablespoons chopped fresh chives or scallion tops

1. Put the potatoes in a medium saucepan of salted water. Bring to a boil. Lower the heat; simmer until almost tender, about 5 minutes. Drain.

2. In a large nonstick or cast-iron frying pan, cook the bacon until crisp. Remove the bacon from the pan and crumble it. Pour off and reserve all but 1 tablespoon of the fat from the pan. Add the onion to the pan and cook over moderate heat, stirring frequently, until browned, about 8 minutes. Remove the onion. Wipe out the pan.

3. In the same pan, heat the reserved bacon fat and enough oil to measure 3 tablespoons over moderately high heat. Add the potatoes; let them cook, without stirring, for 6 minutes. Add ¼ teaspoon of the salt, stir, and cook the potatoes until well browned, about 6 minutes longer. Add the onion and bacon and continue cooking until they are warm through, about 1 minute longer.

4. In a medium saucepan, heat the cream cheese, milk, Worcestershire sauce, cayenne, and the remaining ¼ teaspoon salt over moderately low heat, stirring, until hot, about 5 minutes. Add the crab and black pepper and cook, stirring, until warm through, about 2 minutes longer. Stir the crab mixture and 2 tablespoons of the chives into the potatoes until just combined. Serve topped with the remaining 1 tablespoon chives.

SHRIMP IN GARLIC SAUCE

Based on a popular Spanish *tapa*, or appetizer, this dish is delicious enough to serve as a main course. You just sauté the shrimp in garlicky, spicy olive oil and then toss them with sherry, lemon juice, and a handful of parsley. The shrimp will be equally good hot or at room temperature.

WINE RECOMMENDATION
Bold Mediterranean flavors welcome an easygoing wine such as a dry rosé from Spain or the south of France. If you prefer a wine with a bit more sweetness, try a white zinfandel from California.

SERVES 4

⅓ cup olive oil

4 cloves garlic, cut into thin slices

1 bay leaf

¼ teaspoon dried red-pepper flakes

2 pounds large shrimp, shelled

1¼ teaspoons salt

¼ teaspoon fresh-ground black pepper

3 tablespoons dry sherry

2 tablespoons lemon juice

3 tablespoons chopped fresh parsley

1. In a large frying pan, heat the oil over moderate heat. Add the garlic, bay leaf, and red-pepper flakes and cook for 3 minutes, stirring occasionally.

2. Add the shrimp, salt, and black pepper to the pan and stir to combine. Cook, stirring occasionally, until the shrimp are just done, 4 to 5 minutes. Stir in the sherry, lemon juice, and parsley.

FISH ALTERNATIVES

Squid would be delicious with the garlic sauce. Cook it quickly (for about two minutes), or it will become tough and rubbery. Sea scallops are another alternative; cook them for about two minutes per side, without stirring, so they brown nicely.

DEVEINING SHRIMP

Dark shrimp veins are usually removed for aesthetic purposes. We find that it's not essential to take them out, especially if you're pressed for time.

SHRIMP ENCHILADAS

Feel free to experiment with the filling for these festive Mexican-style packets. Use cheddar cheese instead of Jack. Replace the black beans with pinto beans. Vary the spiciness simply by choosing the ready-made salsa that's right for your palate.

WINE RECOMMENDATION
Beer is always a safe bet with Mexican food. But think about trying a glass of cold rosé, such as a white zinfandel or the drier vin gris from California.

SERVES 4

- 4 tablespoons cooking oil
- 1 pound medium shrimp, shelled
- ¼ teaspoon salt
- ⅛ teaspoon fresh-ground black pepper
- 8 6-inch flour tortillas
- 1⅔ cups drained and rinsed black beans (one 15-ounce can)
- ¼ pound Monterey Jack cheese, grated (about 1 cup)
- 2 cups chunky tomato salsa (one 16-ounce jar)
- ½ cup sour cream
- 2 teaspoons chopped fresh chives or scallion tops

1. Heat the oven to 250°. Cover a baking sheet with paper towels. In a large heavy frying pan, heat 1 tablespoon of the oil over moderately high heat. Sprinkle the shrimp with the salt and pepper. Put the shrimp in the pan and cook, stirring, until just done, about 4 minutes. Remove the shrimp from the pan.

2. Lay the tortillas on a work surface. Cover half of each with the beans. Top with the cheese and then the shrimp. Fold the tortillas in half.

3. In the frying pan, heat the remaining 3 tablespoons oil over moderately high heat. Add four enchiladas and brown, about 30 seconds per side. Put on the baking sheet and keep warm in the oven. Repeat with the remaining enchiladas.

4. Drain the oil from the frying pan and then return four of the enchiladas to the pan. Put the rest in a second frying pan. Over moderate heat, add half the salsa to each pan and cook until the tortillas are slightly softened, turning once, about 2 minutes in all. Serve the enchiladas topped with dollops of sour cream and the chives.

FISH ALTERNATIVES

If available, crawfish tails, often sold already cooked, would be fantastic here. Or you can buy cooked shrimp to save yourself a step.

FRIED-CATFISH SANDWICHES WITH SPICY MAYONNAISE

Moist, juicy catfish, coated with cornmeal and fried crisp, makes a delicious sandwich on a crusty roll with peppery mayonnaise. If you're not in a sandwich mood, skip the roll, but don't hold the mayo: It makes a fine dipping sauce for the fish.

WINE RECOMMENDATION

These laid-back catfish sandwiches will be great with beer or with a straightforward, gulpable red wine. Choose a gamay from California or a Beaujolais from France, which is also made from the gamay grape. Chill the wine slightly for maximum enjoyment.

SERVES 4

½ cup mayonnaise

¾ teaspoon fresh-ground black pepper

⅛ teaspoon cayenne

4 large crusty rolls, split

¾ cup cornmeal

1¼ teaspoons salt

½ teaspoon dried thyme

2 pounds catfish fillets

2 eggs, beaten to mix

¼ cup cooking oil

3 cups tender greens, such as spinach or leaf lettuce (about 2 ounces)

1. In a small bowl, combine the mayonnaise, ½ teaspoon of the black pepper, and the cayenne. Spread the mayonnaise mixture on the rolls.

2. In a shallow bowl, combine the cornmeal with the salt, thyme, and the remaining ¼ teaspoon black pepper. Dip the fillets into the beaten eggs and then into the seasoned cornmeal. Shake off the excess cornmeal.

3. In a large nonstick frying pan, heat the oil over moderate heat. Add the cornmeal-coated fish and fry, turning once, until golden on the outside and just done in the center, about 4 minutes per side for ¾-inch-thick fillets. Drain the fish on paper towels. Sandwich the catfish and greens in the rolls.

FISH ALTERNATIVES

Substitute moderately firm, lean fillets for the catfish. Scrod, rockfish, ocean perch, haddock, or tilefish are good options.

CRISP WHOLE RED SNAPPER WITH ASIAN CITRUS SAUCE

A whole red snapper, its skin delectably crunchy from sizzling in hot oil, is an Asian classic that is not to be missed. Be sure to serve the fish with plenty of steamed rice.

WINE RECOMMENDATION

A crisp, acidic white wine will be best with the citrus flavors and Asian ingredients of this dish. Try a sauvignon blanc from the Loire Valley in France (Sancerre) or a pinot blanc from the Alsace region.

SERVES 4

2 whole red snappers (1½ to 1¾ pound each), cleaned and scaled

Cooking oil, for frying

6 tablespoons canned low-sodium chicken broth or homemade stock

2 tablespoons plus 2 teaspoons soy sauce

2 tablespoons lime juice

4 teaspoons fresh orange juice

2 teaspoons Asian sesame oil

½ teaspoon grated fresh ginger

2 scallions including green tops, cut into thin slices

1. Rinse the fish and dry the surface and the cavity of each thoroughly with paper towels. In a 12-inch or larger nonstick frying pan, heat ⅜ of an inch of cooking oil over moderately high heat until very hot. A deep-fat thermometer should register 375°. Carefully add the fish, let-ting the tails stick out of the pan if necessary. Let the fish cook, without moving them, until crisp and browned, about 9 minutes. Using a large spatula, carefully turn each fish. Continue cooking until crisp and browned and just done, about 7 minutes longer. Drain on paper towels.

2. Meanwhile, in a small glass or stainless-steel bowl, combine the broth, soy sauce, lime juice, orange juice, sesame oil, grated ginger, and scallions.

3. Serve the fish on a platter. Run a knife between the flesh and the bones and lift off the fillet with the skin attached. Turn the fish over and repeat. Pass the sauce.

FISH ALTERNATIVES

In place of the whole red snappers, you can use whole sea bass, porgies, or rockfish of the same weight.

BEER-BATTERED COD WITH TARTAR SAUCE

For a crackling crisp coating, fry the cod in small batches. Too many pieces in the pot cool the oil, and the fish comes out soggy and greasy instead of great.

WINE RECOMMENDATION
Beer is a natural choice to drink with fried fish. If you opt to drink wine, look for one that will mimic beer's palate-cleansing qualities. Try a reasonably priced sparkling wine or an acidic white such as a pinot grigio from Italy.

SERVES 4

1   cup mayonnaise

1   tablespoon Dijon mustard

1   scallion including green top, chopped

1½ teaspoons lemon juice

2   tablespoons chopped dilled gherkins

1   tablespoon chopped capers

2   tablespoons chopped fresh parsley

   Salt

   Fresh-ground black pepper

   Cooking oil, for frying (approximately 1 quart)

1   cup flour

1   egg, beaten to mix

1   cup beer

2   pounds cod fillets, cut into approximately 1½-by-3-inch pieces

1. In a medium bowl, combine the mayonnaise, mustard, scallion, lemon juice, gherkins, capers, parsley, and a pinch each of salt and pepper. Heat the oven to 200°. Cover a baking sheet with paper towels and top with a rack.

2. In a medium pot, heat 3 inches of oil to approximately 365°. Meanwhile, in a medium bowl, combine the flour with ½ teaspoon salt. Whisk in the egg. Add the beer slowly, whisking.

3. Dip the pieces of cod, a few at a time, in the batter, and then put them in the oil. Cook until the fish is done and the crust is light brown, about 4 minutes for ¾-inch thick fillets. Remove the fish with tongs and put the pieces on the rack to drain. Sprinkle salt over the hot fish and put the baking sheet in the oven. Repeat in batches with the remaining fish. Serve with the tartar sauce.

THE COD CLAN

Atlantic pollack, haddock, and hake are among the members of the extensive cod family. Although these fish vary slightly in terms of texture and flavor, one can generally be substituted for another. Small cod are often called scrod and can certainly be used here.

CHAPTER FIVE

Braised, Steamed, Boiled & Poached

COD WITH TOMATO GINGER SAUCE

Though you can put this simple tomato sauce together in a matter of minutes, it has a surprisingly complex flavor. The sauce will seem thick, but the juices that come from the fish during cooking will thin it to just the right consistency.

WINE RECOMMENDATION

Look for an acidic white without too much personality, so the wine won't get in the way of the tomato ginger sauce. Try a Portuguese vinho verde or a refreshing French Côtes de Gascogne.

SERVES 4

- 1 tablespoon cooking oil
- 1 onion, chopped
- 1½ teaspoons grated fresh ginger
- 1¾ cups canned crushed tomatoes in thick puree
- ¾ teaspoon salt
- 2 pounds cod or scrod fillets, cut to make 4 pieces
- ¼ teaspoon fresh-ground black pepper
- ¼ cup chopped cilantro or parsley

1. In a large deep frying pan, heat the oil over moderately low heat. Add the onion and cook, stirring occasionally, until starting to soften, about 3 minutes. Stir in the ginger; cook, stirring, 2 minutes longer. Add the tomatoes and salt and bring to a simmer. Reduce the heat to low and cook, covered, for 10 minutes.

2. Add the fillets and black pepper to the pan and cook, covered, until just done, 10 to 12 minutes longer for 1-inch thick fillets. Stir the cilantro into the sauce. Serve the fish topped with the sauce.

FISH ALTERNATIVES

Other relatively firm, thick fillets or steaks that would be good include orange roughy, grouper, and halibut.

VARIATION

COD WITH SPICY TOMATO GINGER SAUCE

Add 1 chopped jalapeño pepper to the sauce along with the fresh ginger.

Spanish Braised Monkfish

Olive oil, red bell peppers, garlic, and sherry give this gently simmered fish its Spanish accent. They're pureed with another favorite Spanish ingredient, blanched almonds, which thicken the sauce and give it a sweet, nutty flavor.

WINE RECOMMENDATION

A fresh, fruity but not-too-sweet rosé will complement the Mediterranean flavors here. Look for a rosé from Rioja to carry out the Spanish theme, or try one from southern France.

SERVES 4

- 2 tablespoons olive oil
- 1 onion, chopped
- 2 red bell peppers, diced
- 1½ teaspoons salt
- 3 cloves garlic, minced
- ⅓ cup dry sherry
- 1 cup bottled clam juice
- ¼ cup blanched slivered almonds
- ½ teaspoon fresh-ground black pepper
- 2 pounds monkfish, membranes removed, fish cut to make 4 pieces
- 2 tablespoons chopped fresh parsley

1. In a large deep frying pan, heat the oil over moderate heat. Add the onion, bell peppers, and salt and cook, stirring occasionally, until the onion is soft, about 5 minutes. Stir in the garlic and sherry; simmer for 1 minute. Add the clam juice and bring to a simmer. Reduce the heat and simmer, covered, for 10 minutes.

2. Transfer the contents of the frying pan to a blender or food processor and puree. Add the almonds and the black pepper. Pulse until the nuts are chopped very fine. Return the sauce to the pan.

3. Bring the sauce just to a simmer and add the fish to the pan. Simmer, covered, until just done, 10 to 12 minutes. Slice the fish on the diagonal and serve with the parsley sprinkled over the top.

Fish Alternatives

Though monkfish is quite firm, a relatively firm, thick white fish, such as haddock, cod, or halibut, would also be delicious braised in this flavorful sauce.

TILAPIA WITH
TOMATO AND ARTICHOKE SAUCE

A fast tomato sauce with garlic, rosemary, and red wine acts as a perfect braising medium for tilapia, a lean white fish now farmed and readily available. Chopped artichoke hearts and a sprinkling of fresh parsley or basil complete the sauce. For a bolder flavor, toss in some capers or chopped black olives at the end.

WINE RECOMMENDATION
The acidity in the tomatoes makes this a good candidate for pairing with an assertive, acidic white wine with plenty of character. A sauvignon blanc, either from the Loire Valley in France (such as a Sancerre) or from California, would be a good choice.

SERVES 4

1	tablespoon cooking oil
4	cloves garlic, minced
½	cup red wine
2½	cups canned crushed tomatoes in thick puree (from one 28-ounce can)
1¼	teaspoons dried rosemary
1¼	teaspoons salt
½	teaspoon fresh-ground black pepper
2	pounds tilapia fillets
1½	cups chopped drained and rinsed artichoke hearts (one 14½-ounce can)
2	tablespoons chopped fresh parsley or basil

1. In a large deep frying pan, heat the oil over moderately low heat. Add the garlic and cook, stirring, until fragrant, about 1 minute.

Stir in the wine, tomatoes, rosemary, ¾ teaspoon of the salt, and ¼ teaspoon of the pepper. Bring to a simmer and continue simmering, covered, for 10 minutes.

2. Sprinkle the fillets with the remaining ½ teaspoon salt and ¼ teaspoon pepper. Nestle the fish in the sauce, bring back to a simmer, and continue simmering gently, covered, until just done, about 6 minutes for ½-inch-thick fillets.

3. Carefully remove the fish from the pan. Stir the artichoke hearts and parsley into the sauce and cook until warmed through, about 2 minutes. Stir in any accumulated juices from the fish. Spoon the sauce over the tilapia.

FISH ALTERNATIVES

Cod, haddock, grouper, and Chilean sea bass fillets would all work well in this recipe.

CURRIED SCALLOPS WITH SPINACH

With few ingredients and even fewer steps, this curry is a cinch to make quickly. Most of the work is done by a blender, which ensures a silky sauce. If you don't have a blender, use a food processor; the texture will just be slightly less smooth.

WINE RECOMMENDATION

Sauvignon blanc is a perfect choice to serve with this dish. Its acidity will go well with the spinach and work beautifully with both the mild curry and the scallops. You'll find good possibilities from many continents: Try a bottle from California, New Zealand, or South Africa.

SERVES 4

- 2 tablespoons butter
- 1 onion, chopped
- ½ teaspoon salt
- 2 teaspoons curry powder
- 2 teaspoons tomato paste
- ½ cup canned low-sodium chicken broth or homemade stock
- 1 cup light cream or half-and-half
- 2 cups shredded spinach (about 3 ounces spinach leaves)
- 2 pounds sea scallops

1. In a large frying pan, melt the butter over moderately low heat. Add the onion and salt and cook, stirring occasionally, until the onion starts to soften, about 3 minutes. Stir in the curry powder and cook for 1 minute.

2. Transfer the onion mixture to a blender and add the tomato paste, broth, and cream. Puree until smooth. Return the sauce to the pan.

3. Bring the curry sauce just to a simmer. Stir in the spinach and scallops. Simmer, covered, until the scallops are just done, 5 to 7 minutes.

FISH ALTERNATIVES

Shelled medium shrimp would be delicious simmered in the curry sauce. You can also use bay scallops instead of the larger sea scallops, in which case reduce the cooking time to three minutes.

SHRIMP ÉTOUFFÉE

We've played with the traditional étouffée method a bit to make our recipe quick. But this version of the Acadian classic—shrimp smothered in a roux-thickened sauce of vegetables and spices—is every bit as luscious as the original. For extra heat, add more cayenne or a touch of Tabasco sauce.

WINE RECOMMENDATION
The down-home taste of this American original is perfect with a refreshing American white wine. Try a pinot gris from Oregon or a dry riesling, either from Oregon or Washington State. All of these have more acidity than their California counterparts.

SERVES 4

2   tablespoons cooking oil

2   tablespoons flour

1½ cups canned low-sodium chicken broth or homemade stock

1   green bell pepper, chopped

2   ribs celery, chopped

2   onions, chopped

1   bay leaf

2   teaspoons salt

¼   teaspoon cayenne

½   teaspoon fresh-ground black pepper

½   teaspoon dried thyme

1½ pounds medium shrimp, shelled

2   scallions including green tops, chopped

    Boiled or steamed rice, for serving

1. In a large frying pan or Dutch oven, heat the oil over moderate heat until almost smoking. Add the flour and whisk until it's the color of peanut butter, about 3 minutes. Whisk in the broth and continue whisking until the sauce starts to thicken, about 2 minutes.

2. Stir in the bell pepper, celery, onions, bay leaf, salt, cayenne, black pepper, and thyme. Bring to a simmer, cover, and cook over low heat until the vegetables are tender, about 15 minutes.

3. Add the shrimp and scallions and simmer until the shrimp are just done, about 3 minutes. Serve the étouffée over the rice.

FISH ALTERNATIVES

The most authentic substitution, if you can get them, would be cooked crawfish tails. Toss them in at the end and just heat through.

STEAMED ORANGE ROUGHY WITH MUSHROOM SAUCE

Seared mushrooms top steamed orange roughy and are topped in turn with an Asian combination of ginger, scallions, garlic, soy sauce, and dry mustard. The mustard both thickens the sauce and gives it an appealing bite.

WINE RECOMMENDATION
An acidic, medium-bodied white wine is the best choice to pair with the spicy, salty Asian flavors in this dish. Try a wine made from a Loire Valley chenin blanc, such as Vouvray.

SERVES 4

- 2 pounds orange-roughy fillets, cut to make 4 pieces
- ¾ teaspoon salt
- ½ teaspoon fresh-ground black pepper
- 2 tablespoons plus 1 teaspoon cooking oil
- 1 pound mushrooms, cut into thin slices
- 2 teaspoons chopped fresh ginger
- 2 scallions including green tops, cut into ½-inch pieces
- 3 cloves garlic, minced
- 2 tablespoons soy sauce
- 1¾ teaspoons dry mustard
- ¼ cup dry white wine or sherry
- ½ cup canned low-sodium chicken broth or homemade stock

1. In a large pot, bring about 1 inch of water to a boil. Sprinkle the fish with ½ teaspoon of the salt and ¼ teaspoon of the pepper. Fold each fillet in half and put the fillets in a steamer basket over the boiling water. Reduce the heat to moderately high, cover, and steam until just done, about 10 minutes for folded ½-inch-thick fillets. Transfer the fillets to plates.

2. Meanwhile, in a large frying pan, heat the 2 tablespoons oil over high heat. Add the mushrooms and the remaining ¼ teaspoon each of salt and pepper. Cook until browned, about 5 minutes. Top the fish with the mushrooms.

3. Reduce the heat to moderately low. Heat the remaining teaspoon of oil in the pan; add the ginger, scallions, and garlic. Cook, stirring, for 1 minute. Stir in the soy sauce, dry mustard, wine, and broth. Simmer, stirring occasionally, until slightly thickened, about 2 minutes. Spoon the sauce over the mushrooms and fish.

FISH ALTERNATIVES

Steam fillets of sole, whitefish, or turbot to pair with the mushroom sauce. If the fillets are thin, either fold them in half or roll them up before steaming.

STEAMED SALMON WITH WATERCRESS AND LEMON BUTTER

Steaming keeps fish moist and couldn't be quicker. Here watercress is steamed with the salmon, and both benefit from a spoonful of lemon butter. You could use olive oil instead of the butter, however, or just serve lemon wedges.

WINE RECOMMENDATION
The pleasures of red wine with fish are most compelling when a light, fruity red wine is paired with salmon. Choose either a California or Oregon pinot noir or a modestly priced red Burgundy (made from pinot noir).

SERVES 4

- 2 pounds center-cut salmon fillet, cut into 4 pieces
- ¾ teaspoon salt
  Fresh-ground black pepper
- 1 bunch watercress, tough stems removed
- 4 tablespoons butter
- ¾ teaspoon lemon juice

1. In a large pot, bring about 1 inch of water to a boil. Put the fish in a large steamer basket, skin-side down; sprinkle with ¼ teaspoon of the salt and ¼ teaspoon pepper. Pile the watercress on top. Sprinkle with another ¼ teaspoon salt.

2. Put the steamer basket with the fish over the boiling water and cover. Reduce the heat to moderately high and cook until the watercress is wilted and the salmon is just barely done (the fish should still be translucent in the center), about 5 minutes for a 1-inch-thick fillet.

3. Meanwhile, in a small stainless-steel saucepan, melt the butter. Add the lemon juice, the remaining ¼ teaspoon salt, and a pinch of pepper. Serve the salmon and watercress topped with the lemon butter.

FISH ALTERNATIVE

Use halibut fillets instead of salmon. Steaks from either fish will work, too; a one-inch-thick steak takes the same time to cook.

REMOVING PIN BONES

Many types of fish fillets have a line of small bones running the whole length just to one side of the center. Run your finger down the fillet to find them. The best way to remove these bones is with long-nosed pliers. Don't worry if you don't have the time, though. The bones are much easier to remove as you eat, when the flesh is cooked.

139

SHRIMP, JICAMA, AND MANGO SALAD

The crunchy jicama and the soft, sweet mango provide lively counterpoints to the shrimp in both flavor and texture. Tossed with a lemony vinaigrette and a generous amount of cilantro, the salad is ideal for a warm summer evening.

WINE RECOMMENDATION

Mango, lemon juice, and cilantro invite a light-bodied, acidic white, such as an Orvieto from Italy or a Muscadet de Sèvre-et-Maine from France.

SERVES 4

¾ cup water

2 teaspoons salt

1½ pounds large shrimp, shelled

1 small jicama (about ¾ pound), peeled and cut into ¼-inch dice

1 mango, peeled and cut into ¼-inch dice

½ cup chopped cilantro or flat-leaf parsley

6 tablespoons lemon juice

½ teaspoon Dijon mustard

¼ teaspoon fresh-ground black pepper

¼ cup olive oil

1. In a large frying pan, bring the water and ¾ teaspoon of the salt to a boil. Add the shrimp, cover, and bring back to a boil. Cook, covered, over moderate heat for 1 minute. Stir. Continue cooking until the shrimp are just done, about 2 minutes longer. Drain. When the shrimp are cool enough to handle, cut each one in half lengthwise and then in half crosswise.

2. Put the shrimp in a large glass or stainless-steel bowl and add the jicama, mango, and cilantro.

3. In a small glass or stainless-steel bowl, whisk together the lemon juice, the mustard, the remaining 1¼ teaspoons of salt, and the pepper. Add the oil slowly, whisking. Just before serving, add this vinaigrette to the shrimp mixture and toss.

SHELLFISH ALTERNATIVES

Crabmeat, though expensive, is delicious in this salad and is a time-saver, too, since it's usually already cooked. (For that matter, you can use precooked shrimp instead of boiling uncooked ones.) If you really want to splurge, try the salad with lobster; see page 183 for boiling tips.

SHRIMP BOIL WITH SPICY BUTTER SAUCE

Shell the shrimp right at the table and then dunk each one into our positively addictive cayenne-spiced sauce. For tamer tastes, serve the shrimp with lemon wedges instead.

WINE RECOMMENDATION
Pop open a cold beer for this one, or be adventurous and try pairing the spiciness of the shrimp boil with a palate-cleansing, refreshing sparkling wine from California or Australia.

SERVES 4

1½ quarts water

¼ cup vinegar

½ lemon, cut into thin slices

2 cloves garlic, smashed

5 tablespoons Old Bay Seasoning

½ teaspoon peppercorns

1½ teaspoons salt

1¼ teaspoons cayenne

4 bay leaves, crumbled

2 pounds large shrimp, in their shells

½ pound butter

4 teaspoons Worcestershire sauce

2 teaspoons lemon juice

1. In a large pot, combine the water, vinegar, lemon slices, garlic, Old Bay Seasoning, peppercorns, ½ teaspoon of the salt, ¼ teaspoon of the cayenne, and the bay leaves. Cover and bring to a boil. Reduce the heat and simmer for 5 minutes.

2. Add the shrimp to the pot. Cover and bring back to a boil. Then continue boiling, partially covered, until the shrimp are just done, 1 to 2 minutes. Drain.

3. In a small stainless-steel saucepan, melt the butter. Remove the pan from the heat and add the Worcestershire sauce, the lemon juice, and the remaining 1 teaspoon salt and 1 teaspoon cayenne. Divide the sauce among four small bowls. Serve the shrimp with the butter dipping sauce.

BOILED LOBSTER WITH PEPPER BUTTER

Have something to celebrate? Treat yourself to a dinner of boiled lobster with warm butter dipping sauce. You won't have to spend much time in the kitchen—this is one of the quickest of all our recipes to prepare.

WINE RECOMMENDATION
An expansive chardonnay with or without oak flavor is ideal with lobster. Try a bottle from California or Australia. Or, if you really want to celebrate, select a Meursault premier cru (made from chardonnay) from the Burgundy region of France.

SERVES 4

4   lobsters (about 1½ pounds each)
½   pound butter
4½ teaspoons lemon juice
¼   cup chopped fresh parsley
1   teaspoon salt
2   teaspoons fresh-ground black pepper

1.   In a large pot of boiling, salted water, cook the lobsters, covered, until just done, about 10 minutes after the water returns to a boil.

2.   Meanwhile, in a medium stainless-steel saucepan, melt the butter. Remove the pan from the heat and add the lemon juice, parsley, salt, and pepper. Divide the butter among four small bowls. Serve the lobsters with the pepper butter for dipping.

HOW TO EAT A LOBSTER

■ Twist off the "arms" of the lobster and break off the claws. Bend the "thumb" of each claw down until it cracks. Using a lobster cracker, break the claw shells and gently extract the meat with a small fork. Crack the "arms" and extract the meat with the fork.

■ Using your hands, break the lobster in half at the point where the body meets the tail. The tomalley, the soft green part in the body, is good to eat, and you can easily spoon it out. You can also eat the bright red roe, if any, at the body-end of the tail.

■ Using your hands, squeeze the sides of the tail together so that the underside cracks. With the underside facing you, and one hand on each side of the shell, press open the tail exposing the meat; extract it with the fork.

■ There is a little meat in the legs. If you like, twist them off, break them in half, and suck out the meat.

SKATE WITH CAPERS AND BROWN BUTTER

Long a French favorite, skate is becoming increasingly popular with American cooks as they discover just how moist, succulent, and flavorful it is. Ours is a classic French preparation—poached with herbs and sauced with a combination of pungent capers, vinegar, and mellow browned butter. Boiled potatoes are the classic accompaniment.

WINE RECOMMENDATION
Capers suggest a medium-bodied, flavorful white wine, such as a Gavi from Italy or a pinot blanc from Alsace in France.

SERVES 4

4 pieces skate wing, unfilleted (about 2½ pounds in all)

4½ cups water, or more if needed

½ cup plus 1½ tablespoons red-wine vinegar

1 teaspoon dried thyme

1¾ teaspoons salt

¼ teaspoon peppercorns

2 bay leaves

¼ pound butter

⅓ cup capers

¼ cup chopped flat-leaf parsley

⅛ teaspoon fresh-ground black pepper

1. Put the skate in a large deep frying pan in one layer. Pour the water and the ½ cup vinegar over the fish. Add the thyme, 1 teaspoon of the salt, the peppercorns, bay leaves, and more water if needed to cover. Bring to a simmer and cook, partially covered, at a gentle simmer for 3 minutes. Raise the heat and bring to a rolling boil.

Remove from the heat and let sit until the fish is just done, about 5 minutes. Carefully remove the fish and drain on paper towels.

2. Meanwhile, in a medium stainless-steel saucepan, melt the butter over moderate heat. Cook until the butter turns a medium brown, about 5 minutes. Remove from the heat and carefully stir in the remaining 1½ tablespoons vinegar, the capers, the parsley, the remaining ¾ teaspoon salt, and the ground pepper. Serve the fish topped with the sauce.

POACHED SALMON WITH CUCUMBER RAITA

Gently simmering salmon in a flavorful white-wine broth is a classic cooking method that gives the fish a delicious flavor and a delicate texture. Serve this hot or at room temperature. *Raita*, the cooling condiment served in India, makes a superb sauce.

WINE RECOMMENDATION
To match the acidity of the yogurt and the richness of the fish, look for a white that blends crisp acidity with good body. Try a pinot gris from Oregon or a sauvignon blanc from New Zealand.

SERVES 4

1½   quarts water

1½   cups dry white wine

3   tablespoons vinegar

1   onion, sliced

1   carrot, sliced

9   sprigs parsley

¾   teaspoon dried thyme

¼   teaspoon peppercorns

3   bay leaves

3¼   teaspoons salt

1   cucumber, peeled, seeded, and grated

1¾   cups plain yogurt

1   clove garlic, minced

2   tablespoons chopped fresh mint

¼   teaspoon fresh-ground black pepper

2   pounds center-cut salmon fillet, cut into 4 pieces

⅛   teaspoon paprika

1. In a large deep frying pan, combine the water, wine, vinegar, onion, carrot, parsley, thyme, peppercorns, bay leaves, and 2¼ teaspoons of the salt. Cover and bring to a boil over high heat. Reduce the heat and simmer, partially covered, for 10 minutes.

2. Meanwhile, in a medium glass or stainless-steel bowl, combine the cucumber and the remaining teaspoon salt. Let sit for 10 minutes. With your hands, squeeze the cucumber and discard the liquid. Put the cucumber back into the bowl and add the yogurt, garlic, mint, and ground pepper. Refrigerate until ready to serve.

3. Add the fish to the liquid in the pan and bring back to a simmer. Simmer, partially covered, until the fish is just barely done (it should still be translucent in the center), about 4 minutes for a 1-inch-thick fillet. Remove the pan from the heat and let the fish sit in the liquid for 2 minutes. Transfer to plates and, if you like, remove the skin. Serve the salmon warm or at room temperature. Top with the *raita* and then sprinkle the *raita* with the paprika.

MACKEREL VIN BLANC

In the traditional French version of this dish, mackerel fillets are poached in a flavorful white-wine and vinegar broth and served cold as a first course. Here we suggest them as a hot main dish, with the broth and vegetables. Crusty bread is the only accompaniment you'll need.

WINE RECOMMENDATION

Look for something acidic and refreshing to drink alongside this rich fish. Try a bottle of white wine from the Loire Valley in France—either a Muscadet de Sèvre-et-Maine or a slightly more full-bodied Sancerre or other wine made from sauvignon blanc grapes.

SERVES 4

- 2 cups dry white wine
- 3 tablespoons wine vinegar
- 3 tablespoons olive oil
- 2 onions, cut in half lengthwise and then crosswise into thin slices
- 1 carrot, cut into thin slices
- 1 clove garlic, smashed
- 3/4 teaspoon dried thyme
- 1/2 teaspoon coriander seeds
- 8 peppercorns
- 8 sprigs parsley
- 2 bay leaves
- 1 1/4 teaspoons salt
- 2 pounds mackerel fillets
- 1/4 teaspoon fresh-ground black pepper

1. In a medium stainless-steel saucepan, combine the wine, vinegar, oil, onions, carrot, garlic, thyme, coriander, peppercorns, parsley, bay leaves, and salt. Cover and bring to a boil. Reduce the heat to moderately low and cook for 10 minutes.

2. Oil a heavy flameproof 9-by-13-inch stainless-steel or enamel pan. Put the fish, skin-side down, in the pan in an even layer. Pour the hot wine broth on the fish, spread the vegetables over the fillets in an even layer, and sprinkle with the ground pepper. Cover with aluminum foil and bring to a simmer over moderately high heat. Reduce the heat and cook at a gentle simmer until the fish is just done, about 10 minutes for 1/2-inch-thick fillets. Remove the parsley and bay leaves. Serve in shallow bowls.

FISH ALTERNATIVE

Another flavorful fish such as bluefish or shad would be good here. Because these fillets are thicker, you'll need to poach them a few minutes longer.

CHAPTER SIX

Pasta, Rice & Couscous

SALMON AND WHOLE-WHEAT NOODLES IN GINGER BROTH

The fish and noodles here have just enough broth to swim in, but not so much that you'd call this a soup. The recipe is inspired by Japanese soba-noodle dishes, so if buckwheat soba noodles are available in your area, use them instead.

WINE RECOMMENDATION
A full-bodied but acidic white wine will be well-suited to the deep, earthy flavors of the whole-wheat noodles, salmon, and mushrooms. Tokay Pinot Gris from the Alsace in France or sémillon from Washington State are both good examples.

SERVES 4

½   pound whole-wheat linguine

2½ cups canned low-sodium chicken broth or homemade stock

¼   cup dry sherry

¼   cup soy sauce

1   2-inch piece fresh ginger, peeled and cut into ¼-inch-thick slices

3   scallions including green tops, cut into thin slices

¼   teaspoon salt

¼   pound shiitake mushrooms, stems removed, caps cut into thin slices

1   pound salmon fillet, skinned, cut into 4 pieces

1   quart spinach leaves (about 3 ounces)

¼   pound bean sprouts (about 1 cup)

1. In a large pot of boiling, salted water, cook the linguine until almost done, about 12 minutes. Drain.

2. In a medium saucepan, combine the broth, sherry, soy sauce, ginger, scallions, and salt. Bring to a simmer and continue simmering, covered, for 5 minutes. Add the mushrooms and the salmon to the broth and simmer, covered, until the fish is just cooked through, about 6 minutes for a ¾-inch-thick fillet. Remove the salmon from the broth.

3. Stir the pasta, spinach, and bean sprouts into the broth. Cover and simmer until the pasta is done, about 3 minutes. Put the linguine and vegetables into serving bowls. Top with the salmon and ladle the ginger broth over the top.

FISH ALTERNATIVES

The sherry, soy sauce, and ginger in the broth would also complement meaty tuna steaks. Try them instead of the salmon.

SPAGHETTI WITH MACKEREL AND PINE NUTS

Since fresh sardines are often hard to find, we used mackerel for this delightful variation on the Sicilian *pasta con le sarde* (pasta with sardines). If you're in a hurry, however, you can revert to sardines—the canned kind. They're surprisingly good here.

WINE RECOMMENDATION
The full-force flavors of this dish—from the sweet raisins and strong mackerel to the dill—need to be paired with a full-flavored, acidic white wine. Try a sauvignon blanc from northern Italy or New Zealand.

SERVES 4

¼ cup golden raisins

2 tablespoons hot water

¾ pound spaghetti

7 tablespoons olive oil

1 pound mackerel fillets

1 teaspoon salt

½ teaspoon fresh-ground black pepper

1 small onion, chopped

¼ cup pine nuts

¼ cup chopped fresh dill

1. Put the raisins and the hot water in a small bowl and leave until the water is absorbed. In a large pot of boiling, salted water, cook the spaghetti until just done, about 12 minutes. Drain the spaghetti.

2. Meanwhile, in a large nonstick frying pan, heat 1 tablespoon of the oil over moderate heat. Sprinkle the mackerel with ¼ teaspoon each of the salt and pepper. Cook the fish until just done, 2 to 3 minutes per side for ½-inch thick fillets. Remove the fish and then wipe out the pan. When the fish is cool enough to handle, discard the skin and flake the fish.

3. In the same pan, heat 1 tablespoon of the oil over moderately low heat. Add the onion and cook, stirring, until starting to soften, about 3 minutes. Add the pine nuts and cook, stirring occasionally, until starting to brown, about 3 minutes. Add the raisins, mackerel, the remaining ¾ teaspoon salt, and ¼ teaspoon pepper. Cook until heated through, about 2 minutes. Toss the mixture with the spaghetti, the remaining 5 tablespoons olive oil, and the dill.

VARIATION

SPAGHETTI WITH SARDINES AND PINE NUTS

In place of the mackerel, add two 3½-ounce cans of boneless, skinless sardine fillets, drained, to the pan for the last 2 minutes of cooking. Break the fillets into flakes with a spoon.

SPAGHETTI WITH SQUID IN TOMATO WINE SAUCE

Inexpensive and easy to prepare, squid deserves a place in your weeknight repertoire. Here, it's gently simmered in a garlicky red-wine tomato sauce and then tossed with pasta for a meal that's quick to put together.

WINE RECOMMENDATION
Given squid's mild flavor, the tomato sauce really dictates which wine to serve with this dish. Accordingly, a light-bodied, acidic red wine such as a young, slightly chilled Chianti will work just fine.

SERVES 4

1 tablespoon cooking oil

3 cloves garlic, minced

1/3 cup red wine

1¾ cups canned crushed tomatoes in thick puree

¾ teaspoon salt

1 pound cleaned squid, bodies cut into ½-inch rings, tentacles cut in half

½ pound spaghetti

1/3 cup chopped fresh basil or parsley

1. In a large saucepan, heat the oil over moderately low heat. Add the garlic and cook, stirring, for 1 minute. Add the wine and simmer 1 minute longer. Stir in the tomatoes and salt and bring to a simmer. Add the squid, cover, and simmer gently until the squid is just tender, about 30 minutes. Do not allow to boil.

2. Meanwhile, in a large pot of boiling, salted water, cook the spaghetti until almost done, about 10 minutes. Drain the pasta.

3. Add the basil and the spaghetti to the sauce and simmer until the pasta is done and has absorbed some of the sauce, about 2 minutes.

FISH ALTERNATIVES

You can substitute medium shelled shrimp for the squid. Cook the tomato sauce, covered, for about twenty minutes. Add the shrimp and cook until just done, about three minutes longer.

TEST-KITCHEN TIPS

Squid must be braised slowly over low heat or cooked briefly over high heat. Anything in between makes rubber bands.

SHRIMP AND SQUID NOODLES

A wealth of flavors and textures—shrimp, squid, strips of cooked egg, and crisp bean sprouts—spark this Asian-accented one-dish meal. Be sure to cook the squid quickly over high heat so that it doesn't toughen. If you like, leave the squid out altogether and use twice the amount of shrimp, or vice versa.

WINE RECOMMENDATION

Salty Asian flavors like these call for a very light-bodied, acidic white wine. Try a vinho verde from Portugal or a Muscadet de Sèvre-et-Maine from the Loire Valley in France.

SERVES 4

- 6 tablespoons canned low-sodium chicken broth or homemade stock
- ¼ teaspoon dried red-pepper flakes
- ¼ cup oyster sauce
- 5 tablespoons dry white wine
- 6 tablespoons soy sauce
- ½ pound linguine
- 4½ tablespoons cooking oil
- ½ pound medium shrimp, shelled
- ¼ teaspoon salt
- ½ pound cleaned squid, bodies cut into ½-inch rings, tentacles cut in half
- 2 eggs, beaten to mix
- ½ pound bean sprouts (about 2 cups)
- 1 bunch chives, cut into 1-inch lengths (about ⅔ cup)

1. In a small bowl, combine the broth, red-pepper flakes, oyster sauce, wine, and soy sauce.

In a large pot of boiling, salted water, cook the linguine until just done, about 12 minutes. Drain the linguine.

2. In a large frying pan or wok, heat 1 tablespoon of the oil over high heat. Sprinkle the shrimp with ⅛ teaspoon of the salt. Add the shrimp to the pan; cook until just done, about 3 minutes. Remove the shrimp. Heat another tablespoon oil over high heat. Sprinkle the squid with the remaining ⅛ teaspoon salt. Add the squid to the pan and cook for 30 seconds. Remove. Heat ½ tablespoon of oil and add the eggs to the pan. Cook, stirring, until set, about 20 seconds. Remove and cut into strips.

3. Heat the remaining 2 tablespoons oil over high heat. Add the linguine, bean sprouts, and the sauce mixture. Cook, stirring, until the sauce thickens slightly, about 2 minutes. Add the shrimp, squid, and eggs. Cook until heated through, about 1 minute longer. Toss with the chives and serve immediately.

LINGUINE WITH RED CLAM SAUCE

You can buy fresh or frozen chopped clams, or get about three dozen shucked cherry-stone clams and chop them yourself. Save the juice from the shucked clams and use it in place of or as part of the bottled clam juice; it may be saltier, so begin with less salt and add more to taste if needed.

WINE RECOMMENDATION
A chilled bottle of rosé, such as one from Provence in southern France or a dry California version, will be perfect with the saltiness of the clams and broth and the acidity of the tomato sauce. Avoid sweeter white zinfandels.

SERVES 4

¼ cup olive oil

4 large cloves garlic, chopped

⅔ cup dry white wine

½ teaspoon dried thyme

Pinch dried red-pepper flakes

3 cups canned crushed tomatoes in thick puree (one 28-ounce can)

1 cup bottled clam juice

1¼ teaspoons salt, more if needed

¾ pound chopped clams, drained (about 1½ cups)

⅓ cup chopped flat-leaf parsley

¼ teaspoon fresh-ground black pepper

¾ pound linguine

1. In a large frying pan, heat the oil over moderately low heat. Add the garlic and cook, stirring, for 1 minute. Add the wine, thyme, and red-pepper flakes; bring to a simmer. Cook until reduced to about ⅓ cup, about 5 minutes.

2. Add the tomatoes, clam juice, and salt. Raise the heat to moderate and bring to a simmer. Cook, stirring occasionally, until thickened, about 10 minutes. Add the clams and bring back to a simmer. Continue simmering until the clams are just done, about 1 minute longer. Stir in the parsley and black pepper. Taste the sauce for salt, and add more if needed.

3. Meanwhile, in a large pot of boiling, salted water, cook the linguine until just done, about 12 minutes. Drain and toss with the sauce.

TEST-KITCHEN TIP

Chopped clams are good, but often the liquid they come in tastes of little more than salt. That's why we recommend draining the chopped clams and using bottled clam juice for the liquid in this dish.

163

ORANGE ROUGHY ON RICE WITH THAI-SPICED COCONUT SAUCE

Prepared Thai curry paste helps a dish develop complex flavor in no time. If you have red paste and would like to use it in place of the yellow, add only one-and-a-half teaspoons.

WINE RECOMMENDATION
The perfumed heat of this dish with its full-bodied coconut sauce makes a cold beer a great companion. If you prefer wine, experiment with a moderately priced sparkling one from California.

SERVES 4

1   cup jasmine or other long-grain rice

1½ cups water

1⅔ cups canned unsweetened coconut milk

2   teaspoons yellow Thai curry paste*

⅓   cup canned low-sodium chicken broth or homemade stock

1   tablespoon Asian fish sauce* or soy sauce

1   teaspoon brown sugar

    Pinch turmeric

¾   teaspoon salt

¼   cup flour

¼   teaspoon fresh-ground black pepper

1½ pounds orange-roughy fillets, cut to make 4 pieces

2   tablespoons cooking oil

⅓   cup cilantro leaves (optional)

4   lime wedges, for serving

    *Available at Asian markets and many supermarkets

1. Rinse the rice until the water runs clear. Put the rice in a small saucepan with the water. Bring to a boil, reduce the heat to low, and cook, covered, for 15 minutes. Remove the pan from the heat and let sit, without removing the lid, for 10 minutes.

2. In a medium saucepan, heat the thick coconut milk from the top of the can over moderate heat. Add the curry paste and cook, stirring, for 3 minutes. Whisk in the remaining coconut milk, the broth, fish sauce, brown sugar, turmeric, and ¼ teaspoon of the salt and bring to a simmer. Cook, stirring frequently, until slightly thickened, about 7 minutes.

3. In a shallow bowl, combine the flour, the remaining ½ teaspoon salt, and the pepper. Coat the fish with the flour mixture and shake off any excess. In a large nonstick frying pan, heat the oil over moderately high heat. Put the fish in the pan, skinned-side down, and cook until golden, about 3 minutes. Turn and continue cooking until just done, about 2 minutes longer for 1-inch-thick fillets. Mound the rice on plates and top with the fish and the sauce. Sprinkle with the cilantro, if using, and serve with the lime wedges.

SHARK KABOBS OVER SPICED CASHEW RICE

Chunks of mako shark perch atop Indian-style rice redolent of cinnamon, bay leaf, mustard seed, clove, and cilantro—a tantalizing combination that's heady but not hot. It's customary to leave the whole spices in the rice, but warn your guests about the cloves; they're overwhelming if you bite into one.

WINE RECOMMENDATION

Try matching this aromatic preparation with that most aromatic of all whites, gewürztraminer. Look for a bottle from Alsace or a slightly less acidic version from California.

SERVES 4

1½   cups basmati or other long-grain rice

2¼   cups water

2   cinnamon sticks

10   cloves

3   bay leaves

⅛   teaspoon turmeric

1½   teaspoons salt

1   tablespoon butter

4   tablespoons cooking oil

2   teaspoons black or yellow mustard seeds

¼   cup chopped, roasted, unsalted cashews

1½   pounds shark steak, about 1 inch thick, cut into 1-inch cubes

1   tablespoon lemon juice

3   cloves garlic, minced

¼   teaspoon fresh-ground black pepper

⅓   cup chopped cilantro or parsley

4   lemon wedges, for serving

1. Rinse the rice until the water runs clear. Put the rice in a medium saucepan with the water, cinnamon sticks, cloves, bay leaves, turmeric, and 1 teaspoon of the salt. Bring to a boil, reduce the heat to low, and cook, covered, for 15 minutes. Remove from the heat and let sit, without removing the lid, for 10 minutes.

2. In a small frying pan, melt the butter with 2 tablespoons of the oil over moderately high heat. Add the mustard seeds and cook, stirring, until they begin to pop, about 30 seconds. Add the cashews; cook, stirring, for 30 seconds longer. Gently stir the cashew mixture into the rice with a fork.

3. Heat a grill pan or large heavy frying pan over moderately high heat. Thread the shark onto four small skewers; rub with the remaining 2 tablespoons oil, the lemon juice, and garlic. Sprinkle with the remaining ½ teaspoon salt and the pepper. Cook the kabobs, turning, until just done, about 8 minutes. Add the cilantro to the rice and mound on plates. Top with the shark kabobs and serve with the lemon wedges.

Mediterranean Rice Salad with Seared Tuna

With its tomato, red bell pepper, black olives, thyme, and tuna, this salad sings of sunny southern France. Boiling the rice rather than steaming it cuts down the cooking time considerably.

WINE RECOMMENDATION
Look for a light, refreshing white wine from the Mediterranean. Either a bottle of the delightful albariño from Galicia in Spain or a Côtes de Gascogne from southwestern France would be appropriate.

SERVES 4

1½ cups long-grain rice

1 small red onion, chopped

1 large tomato, seeded and cut into ½-inch dice

1 red bell pepper, seeds and ribs removed, cut into ½-inch dice

½ cup black olives, such as Kalamata, halved and pitted

3 tablespoons chopped flat-leaf parsley

1 teaspoon dried thyme

3 tablespoons white-wine vinegar

1½ teaspoons Dijon mustard

1 clove garlic, minced

1½ teaspoons salt

¾ teaspoon fresh-ground black pepper

⅓ cup plus 1 tablespoon olive oil

4 tuna steaks, about ½ inch thick (1½ pounds in all)

1. In a large pot of boiling, salted water, cook the rice until just done, about 10 minutes. Drain. Rinse with cold water. Drain thoroughly.

2. In a medium glass or stainless-steel bowl, combine the rice, onion, tomato, bell pepper, olives, parsley, and ½ teaspoon of the thyme. In a small glass or stainless-steel bowl, whisk the vinegar with the mustard, garlic, 1 teaspoon of the salt, and ½ teaspoon of the black pepper. Add the ⅓ cup oil slowly, whisking. Toss this vinaigrette with the rice.

3. Rub the tuna with the remaining 1 tablespoon oil and sprinkle with the remaining ½ teaspoon thyme, ½ teaspoon salt, and ¼ teaspoon black pepper. Heat a grill pan or large heavy frying pan over moderately high heat. Put the tuna in the pan and cook for 2 minutes. Turn and cook until done to your taste, about 2 minutes longer for medium rare. Mound the rice on plates and top with the tuna.

SHRIMP AND BAY-SCALLOP RISOTTO WITH MUSHROOMS

Fresh and dried mushrooms give this risotto a double dose of earthy flavor. You can use twice the shrimp and no scallops, or the reverse. If you prefer sea scallops, quarter them.

WINE RECOMMENDATION
The full flavor of shrimp is reason enough to drink a full-bodied chardonnay with this dish. Try a bottle from California or Australia.

SERVES 4

½ ounce dried porcini or other dried mushrooms

⅔ cup boiling water

4 cups canned low-sodium chicken broth or homemade stock

2 cups bottled clam juice

1 tablespoon olive oil

1 tablespoon butter

1 onion, chopped

4 cloves garlic, minced

1¼ cups arborio rice

½ pound mushrooms, cut into thin slices

¼ cup dry white wine

1 teaspoon salt

½ pound medium shrimp, shelled

½ pound bay scallops

1. In a small bowl, soak the dried mushrooms in the boiling water until softened, about 15 minutes. Remove the mushrooms and strain their liquid into a medium saucepan through a sieve lined with a paper towel. Rinse the mushrooms well to remove any remaining grit and chop them. Add the broth and clam juice to the mushroom-soaking liquid and bring to a simmer.

2. In a large pot, heat the oil and butter over moderately low heat. Add the onion and cook, stirring occasionally, until translucent, about 5 minutes. Add the garlic and rice and stir until the rice begins to turn opaque, about 2 minutes. Add the fresh mushrooms and cook for 1 minute. Add the wine and salt and cook, stirring, until the wine has been absorbed.

3. Stir in the dried mushrooms and ½ cup of the simmering stock; cook, stirring frequently, until the stock has been absorbed. The rice and the stock should bubble gently; adjust the heat as needed. Continue cooking the rice, adding the stock ½ cup at a time and allowing the rice to absorb the stock before adding the next ½ cup. Cook the rice until almost tender, about 25 minutes, and then add the shrimp and scallops. Cook, stirring, until the rice is tender and the shrimp and scallops are done, about 5 minutes longer. The stock should be thickened by the starch from the rice. You may not need to use all of the liquid.

Flounder with Herbed Couscous

Parsley puree thinned with lemon juice and oil flavors the couscous and acts as a sauce for the fish. The taste of parsley really comes through if you use the flat-leaf variety.

WINE RECOMMENDATION
Match the tartness of the lemon juice with an acidic white wine. Try a good-quality Soave or Orvieto from Italy.

SERVES 4

- ¾ cup loosely packed flat-leaf parsley leaves
- 2 scallions including green tops, chopped
- 2 teaspoons lemon juice
- 4 tablespoons cooking oil
- 2¼ cups water
- 1¼ teaspoons salt
- ¾ teaspoon fresh-ground black pepper
- 1⅓ cups couscous
- 2 pounds flounder fillets, cut to make 4 pieces
- ¼ cup flour

1. In a blender, puree the parsley and scallions with the lemon juice, 2 tablespoons of the oil, ¼ cup of the water, and ¼ teaspoon each of the salt and pepper.

2. In a medium saucepan, bring the remaining 2 cups water to a boil with ¾ teaspoon of the salt and ¼ teaspoon of the pepper. Stir in 3 tablespoons of the parsley puree and the couscous. Cover, remove from the heat, and let sit for 5 minutes.

3. In a large nonstick frying pan, heat the remaining 2 tablespoons oil over moderately high heat. Sprinkle the fish with the remaining ¼ teaspoon salt and ¼ teaspoon pepper. Dust the flounder with the flour and shake off any excess. Sauté the fish until brown and just done, about 2 minutes a side for ½-inch-thick fillets. Serve the fish on the couscous with the remaining parsley puree on the top.

Fish Alternatives

Any mild-tasting fish fillets will go well with the relatively delicate sauce. Try lake perch, whiting, croaker, drum, or bass, or of course, any of the flounder family, such as lemon or gray sole.

VARIATION

Flounder with Basil and Parsley Couscous

Make the herb puree with ¼ cup fresh basil and ½ cup flat-leaf parsley leaves.

SEA-BASS COUSCOUS

Sweet potatoes, red bell pepper, and chickpeas blend with strips of sea bass in a highly seasoned tomato broth. This satisfying mélange is ladled over a mound of steaming couscous to make a complete meal in one dish.

WINE RECOMMENDATION
The earthy but exotic flavors here invite a cold bottle of rosé. Look for one from Provence in southern France, or, if you like a bit of sweetness, try a white zinfandel from California.

SERVES 4

2   tablespoons cooking oil

1   onion, cut into thin slices

1   red bell pepper, cut into ¾-inch pieces

1   teaspoon paprika

1   teaspoon ground coriander

¼   teaspoon cayenne

½   teaspoon ground ginger

¼   teaspoon cinnamon

½   teaspoon fresh-ground black pepper

2¼ teaspoons salt

1   quart canned low-sodium chicken broth or homemade stock

1   cup canned crushed tomatoes in thick puree

¾   pound sweet potatoes, peeled and cut into ½-inch pieces

2   cups water

1⅓ cups couscous

2   cups drained canned chickpeas, rinsed (from one 19-ounce can)

1   pound sea-bass fillets, skinned, cut into approximately ¾-by-1½-inch pieces

1. In a large pot, heat the oil over moderately low heat. Add the onion and bell pepper and cook, stirring occasionally, until starting to soften, about 4 minutes. Stir in the paprika, coriander, cayenne, ginger, cinnamon, black pepper, and 1 teaspoon of salt. Add the broth, tomatoes, and sweet potatoes. Simmer until the sweet potatoes are almost tender, about 15 minutes.

2. Meanwhile, in a medium saucepan, bring the water and ¾ teaspoon of the salt to a boil. Stir in the couscous. Cover, remove from the heat, and let sit for 5 minutes.

3. Stir the chickpeas, fish, and the remaining ½ teaspoon salt into the sweet-potato mixture. Simmer until the fish is just done, about 4 minutes. Serve the fish and vegetables over the couscous. Ladle the liquid over the top.

FISH ALTERNATIVES

Skinless red snapper, black cod, and tilefish fillets would all be good with this couscous.

Grilled Shrimp with Couscous Salad

A colorful salad of couscous, tomatoes, and watercress makes a tasty bed for skewers of grilled shrimp. If you can't get beautiful summer tomatoes, it's better to leave the tomatoes out. Substitute roasted red bell peppers, if you like.

WINE RECOMMENDATION
Shrimp is often best with a full-bodied white wine, but with all the watercress in this salad you'll want some acidity as well. Try a sémillon from Washington State or a sauvignon blanc from California.

SERVES 4

¼ cup olive oil

½ teaspoon dried tarragon

1 clove garlic, halved

2 pounds large shrimp, shelled

2 cups canned low-sodium chicken broth or homemade stock

1 teaspoon salt

1⅓ cups couscous

2½ cups watercress, tough stems removed (from a 5-ounce bunch)

2 scallions including green tops, chopped

2 tablespoons lemon juice

½ pound tomatoes, diced

½ teaspoon fresh-ground black pepper

Lemon wedges, for serving

1. Light the grill or heat the broiler. In a small saucepan, combine the oil, tarragon, and garlic. Cook over moderately low heat until the garlic just starts to brown, about 3 minutes. Remove from the heat, let the oil cool slightly, and then discard the garlic. Thread the shrimp onto metal or wooden skewers and brush with 1½ tablespoons of the tarragon oil.

2. In a medium saucepan, bring the broth to a boil with ¾ teaspoon of the salt. Stir in the couscous. Cover, remove from the heat, and let sit for 5 minutes. In a large glass or stainless-steel bowl, toss the couscous with the watercress, scallions, lemon juice, tomatoes, and the remaining tarragon oil, ¼ teaspoon salt, and the pepper.

3. Meanwhile, grill or broil the shrimp, turning once, until just done, about 5 minutes. Serve the shrimp skewers on top of the couscous salad with lemon wedges on the side.

Test-Kitchen Tip

Wooden skewers are handy for grilling. Just be sure to soak them in water for at least ten minutes before using, or they could burn.

Fish Facts

Look to this section for practical advice on buying and preparing fish. You'll find: a list of staples to keep on hand for cooking fish; a classification according to season of fish availability; a guide to all the different types of shellfish; and a comparison of wild versus farmed fish.

RECIPES PICTURED OPPOSITE: *(top)* pages 33, 81, 103; *(center)* pages 111, 51, 101; *(bottom)* pages 129, 99, 21.

THE QUICK PANTRY

If you keep basic staples on hand, you can cut shopping to a minimum. Then you'll only have to make one short stop to pick up any fresh vegetables and fish you need to complete the recipe.

CUPBOARD

- artichoke hearts, canned
- beans, canned: black, chickpeas, pinto
- bread crumbs
- chicken broth, low-sodium
- clam juice, bottled
- coconut milk, unsweetened
- cornmeal
- couscous
- garlic
- grape leaves, bottled
- honey
- lentils
- mushrooms, dried
- oil: cooking, olive

- onions
- pasta, dried: linguine, spaghetti
- peppers, bottled: roasted red
- potatoes
- raisins
- rice: arborio, basmati, jasmine, long-grain
- salsa
- shallots
- soy sauce
- Tabasco sauce
- tomatoes: canned, paste, sun-dried
- vinegar: red- or white-wine, white
- Worcestershire sauce

SPICE SHELF

- allspice
- bay leaves
- cayenne
- chili powder
- cinnamon, ground and sticks
- cloves
- coriander, ground and seeds
- cumin
- curry powder
- dill
- fennel seeds
- ginger
- mustard, dry and seeds
- nutmeg
- Old Bay seasoning
- oregano
- paprika
- peppercorns, black
- red-pepper flakes
- rosemary
- sage
- sesame seeds
- tarragon
- thyme
- turmeric

LIQUOR CABINET

- beer
- sherry: dry, sweet
- vermouth, dry
- wine: dry white, red

FREEZER

- bacon
- frozen vegetables: corn, lima beans, peas
- nuts: almonds, cashews, pecans, pine nuts

REFRIGERATOR

- anchovy paste
- butter
- capers
- cheese: cream, feta, Monterey Jack
- cream: heavy, light
- curry paste, Thai yellow
- eggs
- fish sauce, Asian
- ginger, fresh
- gherkins, dilled
- horseradish, bottled
- jalapeño peppers
- lemons
- limes
- mayonnaise
- milk
- mustard: Dijon or grainy
- olives
- oranges
- oyster sauce
- parsley
- pesto
- scallions
- sesame oil, Asian
- sour cream
- tortillas
- yogurt, plain

Seasonal Fish and Shellfish

Most types of fish and shellfish are available fresh year-round. Good freezing techniques and improved shipping have also made it possible for part of the harvest to be frozen and sold throughout the year. Some varieties, however, are only available, are more available, or are at their best and cheapest during certain seasons. To buy those varieties at their peak, refer to the following seasonal list.

Winter
- bay scallops (*Cape Cod and Nantucket waters*)
- bluefish (*Florida coast*)
- king salmon (*Pacific coast*)
- monkfish (*Atlantic and Brazilian coasts*)
- pompano (*Florida coast*)
- shad (*Florida coast*)

Spring
- anchovies (*Mediterranean*)
- monkfish (*Atlantic and Brazilian coasts*)
- pompano (*Florida coast*)
- shad (*mid-Atlantic and North Atlantic coasts*)
- salmon (*Pacific coast*)
- sardines (*Mediterranean*)
- smelts (*all regions*)
- soft-shell crabs (*Florida and mid-Atlantic coasts*)
- whiting (*Atlantic coast*)

Summer
- bluefish (*North Atlantic coast*)
- grouper (*Florida and Gulf coasts*)
- halibut (*mid-Atlantic and North Atlantic coasts*)
- mahimahi (*Atlantic and Pacific coasts*)
- mako shark (*mid-Atlantic and North Atlantic coasts*)
- salmon (*Pacific coast*)
- soft-shell crabs (*mid-Atlantic coast*)
- swordfish (*North Atlantic coast*)
- tuna (*Atlantic and Pacific coasts*)

Fall
- bay scallops (*Long Island waters*)
- coho salmon (*Pacific coast*)
- monkfish (*Atlantic and Brazilian coasts*)
- smelts (*Great Lakes, New York and New England streams*)
- whiting (*Atlantic coast*)
- tuna (*Atlantic and Pacific coasts*)

SHELLFISH PRIMER

CRUSTACEANS

All the members of the crustacean family have external skeletons in the form of outer shells that vary from leathery to firm.

Crab

• **VARIETIES: KING CRABS,** mostly from Alaskan waters, don't have much meat except in the legs, which are sold frozen, already cooked.

DUNGENESS CRABS are large, meaty Pacific coast crabs sold cooked or, locally, live.

BLUE CRABS, popular along the Atlantic coast, are sold live or cooked.

SOFT-SHELL CRABS are blue crabs in their molting stage. These spring and summer treats can be eaten whole, including the shell.

STONE CRABS, from the Gulf coast or Caribbean, have meaty claws that are sold cooked and frozen.

• **BUYING:** Crabs sold raw must be alive. Cooked crabmeat is graded according to the size of the pieces: lump offers the largest pieces, flake contains smaller pieces, and claw meat is completely broken up. Beware of surimi (imitation crabmeat), which resembles the real thing in neither flavor nor texture.

• **STORING:** Since soft-shell crabs can't live long once they're out of the water, don't try to keep them alive in the refrigerator as you would lobsters. Eat them immediately; clean and refrigerate them briefly, not over six hours; or freeze them.

• **PREPARING:** Cooked crabmeat, no matter how expensive, almost always has at least a few bits of shell. Pick through the meat before using it.

Crawfish

• **VARIETIES:** Of the hundreds of species of this fresh-water crustacean (also called **CRAYFISH**), only a few grow large enough to be worth eating. Though similar in appearance, the Louisiana and Pacific Northwest varieties differ in size; the latter are bigger.

• **BUYING:** Purchase the most lively crawfish you can find. Otherwise, buy them frozen or buy the tail meat cooked and shelled.

• **STORING:** Store live crawfish in the refrigerator in a bowl covered with a wet towel for up to twenty-four hours.

• **PREPARING:** Traditionally, the intestinal track is removed while the crawfish is still alive. For the squeamish, it's perfectly acceptable to devein after cooking, or omit this step altogether.

Lobster

• **VARIETIES: AMERICAN, NORTHERN,** or **MAINE LOBSTERS** have the familiar coral and dark greenish-blue shells. The meat, the green tomalley (liver), and the coral (eggs) are all prized.

ROCK or **SPINY LOBSTERS** have no claws; all their meat is in the tail.

• **BUYING:** Buy Maine lobsters alive and kicking. Size does not affect tenderness, and a large one both has more meat and is easier to shell than two small ones. Rock lobsters are usually sold frozen; cold-water sources such as Australia or New Zealand offer the highest quality.

• **STORING:** Refrigerate live lobsters wrapped in wet newspaper for up to a day before cooking.

• **PREPARING:** The easiest way to cook a live lobster is to plunge it into boiling salted water and leave it until the shell turns bright red.

Shrimp

• **VARIETIES:** There are hundreds of tropical, cold-water, and fresh-water species. The last are usually only available locally.

• **BUYING:** Look for firm, fresh-smelling shrimp. They may have bright pink, reddish, gray, or even striped shells. Shrimp that still have their heads are usually the freshest.

• **STORING:** Almost all shrimp in the U.S. arrive at the fish shop frozen and are defrosted for sale. If you don't plan to use the shrimp right away, buy them frozen. Refreezing shrimp will make the meat mealy.

• **PREPARING:** Deveining shrimp is mostly a matter of aesthetics. If you're in a hurry, don't bother.

MOLLUSKS

Clams, mussels, and scallops are bivalves, with two hard shells hinged by a strong muscle. The squid is another type of mollusk, the cephalopod, which has an internal skeleton and no shell. Cephalopods characteristically have tentacles and an ink sac to evade predators.

Clams

• **VARIETIES:** **ATLANTIC HARD-SHELL** or **QUAHOG CLAMS** are sold by size: **littleneck** clams, the smallest and most expensive, are good raw or cooked; **cherrystone** clams are medium-size and good raw or cooked, plain or stuffed; and **chowder** clams, the largest and least expensive, are good cut up in soups.

PACIFIC HARD-SHELL CLAMS include Pacific littlenecks, Manila, pismo, and butter clams.

ATLANTIC SOFT-SHELL CLAMS, also called fryers, steamers, or long-necks, are oval with a protruding neck or siphon extending from one end of the brittle shell.

RAZOR CLAMS, also considered soft-shell, have meat that is quite tough; they're best if you chop them before cooking.

PACIFIC SOFT-SHELL CLAMS or **GEODUCKS** have long necks, usually about ten inches. The meat inside the shell is eaten cooked; the neck is pounded to tenderize it and then fried or sliced paper-thin and eaten raw.

• **BUYING:** Generally, smaller clams are more tender and larger ones are tougher. Discard any that have broken shells, or that don't open after cooking. Hard-shell clams should be closed tightly. Soft-shells can't close completely, and so they're more perishable and sandier than hard-shelled varieties. To check for life, touch the siphon; it should retract toward the shell. Shucked clams should be floating in their own clear liquid.

• STORING: Keep live clams refrigerated in a bowl covered with a wet towel; never store in water.

• PREPARING: Scrub hard-shell clams with a stiff brush under cold running water before using. Soft-shell clams are grittier; before scrubbing, soak them in salted water in the refrigerator for a couple of hours so they can purge excess sand.

Mussels

• VARIETIES: COMMON or BLUE MUSSELS have smooth, blueish-black shells, which should be tightly closed. Like all mussels, these are almost always served cooked.

GREEN LIPPED or NEW ZEALAND MUSSELS have bright-green shells. Expect to pay more for these.

• BUYING: It's important to know the source of your mussels. Your fishmonger should have the certification tag that tells you exactly where the mussels came from. Ask to see it if you have doubts about safety.

• STORING: Keep mussels refrigerated in a bowl covered with a wet towel; never store them in water.

• PREPARING: Discard any mussels whose shells are broken or don't clamp together when tapped. Scrub wild mussels with a stiff brush to remove barnacles; cultivated mussels need only a quick rinse. Pull off the beard before cooking.

Scallops

• VARIETIES: BAY SCALLOPS are small and delicate, with a sweet flavor and a high price tag. **Cape** and **Nantucket** scallops, types of bay scallops, are premium. They're larger than most bay scallops and are exceptionally sweet.

SEA SCALLOPS, the largest variety, are not as sweet as bay, but are still delicious.

CALICO SCALLOPS are very small and have little flavor; they're removed from their shells by steaming, leaving them partially cooked.

SINGING or PINK SCALLOPS, found in the Pacific Northwest, are sold in their shells. The sweet meat is steamed from the shells, as with mussels.

• BUYING: Purchase sweet-smelling specimens with no signs of browning or excess liquid. They should be ivory to pinkish; pure white scallops may have been soaked in tripolyphosphate.

• STORING: If you're fortunate enough to find scallops in their shells, store them in a bowl in the refrigerator, covered with wet paper towels. Use them within a day or two, though, because they die quickly out of the sea.

• PREPARING: A shucked scallop has a small hinge on the side, which originally attached it to its shell. Pull this off before cooking; heat makes it chewy as a rubber band.

Squid

• VARIETIES: Dozens of species exist throughout the world. Both Atlantic and Pacific varieties are available in the U.S.

• BUYING: As with shrimp, most squid has been previously frozen and is sold defrosted. You can almost always buy squid cleaned. Generally, small squid are more tender than large ones.

• STORING: Squid freezes exceptionally well and can even be refrozen.

• PREPARING: So that squid is tender rather than tough and rubbery, cook it very briefly (a minute or two) over high heat or braise slowly (thirty minutes or more) over low heat.

FARM-RAISED FISH

With the increasing demand for fish and shellfish and the dwindling supply from oceans, lakes, and rivers, aquaculture—the farming of fish and shellfish—has grown into a full-fledged industry.

Farming Facts

- **FISH** generally begin life in large tanks and are transferred to ocean or fresh-water pens, where they're fed a steady diet of high-protein pellets.
- **MUSSELS** are grown on stakes, or suspended between the surface of the water and the bottom, and then transferred to beds.
- **SHRIMP** are usually raised in the same way as mussels, though some are grown in sealed-off bays and live on food from the sea.

Farmed vs. Wild

Some people insist that all wild fish is superior to farmed because the flavor is more "natural" and the texture firmer. Yet many people prefer farmed catfish, for instance, specifically because of its milder flavor. Chefs may appreciate the consistent quality of farmed fish, especially those from certain farms located in extremely clean waters. We suggest that you try both wild and farmed fish and see which you like best. You'll probably find, as we have, that you enjoy both and that the occasion and season will determine which you select.

Comparative Characteristics

	WILD	FARMED
FISH	Pronounced flavor	Mild flavor
	Firm, lean	Softer, fattier
	Various sizes	Consistent size
	Often seasonal	Always available
	Expensive	Less expensive
MUSSELS	Rims often tough	Tender
	Various sizes	Consistent size
	Sandy	Clean
SHRIMP	Can be flavorful or bland, firm or mushy, whether wild or farm-raised. Experiment to find the best source near you.	

What's Available

Here are the farm-raised fish and shellfish that you're most likely to find:

- bass, striped
- catfish
- char
- salmon
- sturgeon
- tilapia
- trout
- crawfish
- mussels
- shrimp

INDEX

Page numbers in **boldface** indicate photographs   ❦ indicates wine recommendations